The F
of an
Economic Migrant

À Dennis
avec mes compliments
Yves Benett

a short autobiography
Yves Benett

The Scripture quotations in this book are mostly from the Good News Bible published by Thomas Nelson Inc. under license from the American Bible Society

Note for Librarians: A cataloguing record for this book is available from Library and Archives Canada at www.collectionscanada.ca/amicus/index-e.html
ISBN 1-4251-1684-1

The Cover Photograph (taken by me) shows my family at Flic-en-Flacq, Mauritius, in 1962

Printed in Victoria, BC, Canada. Printed on paper with minimum 30% recycled fibre. Trafford's print shop runs on "green energy" from solar, wind and other environmentally-friendly power sources.

Offices in Canada, USA, Ireland and UK

Book sales for North America and international:
Trafford Publishing, 6E–2333 Government St.,
Victoria, BC V8T 4P4 CANADA
phone 250 383 6864 (toll-free 1 888 232 4444)
fax 250 383 6804; email to orders@trafford.com
Book sales in Europe:
Trafford Publishing (UK) Limited, 9 Park End Street, 2nd Floor
Oxford, UK OX1 1HH UNITED KINGDOM
phone +44 (0)1865 722 113 (local rate 0845 230 9601)
facsimile +44 (0)1865 722 868; info.uk@trafford.com
Order online at:
trafford.com/06-3315

10 9 8 7 6 5 4 3

Yves Benett in 2004, aged 73

DEDICATION
*To all my children and grandchildren, and with deep-felt
gratitude to my wife for her support through all the days
of our life together*

Contents

ACKNOWLEDGEMENT

I would like to express my thanks to my wife Evelyn for her support in so many ways during the years that I was writing this book. I really cannot thank her enough.

The Faith
of an
Economic Migrant

1

Introduction

My Aim

In this brief autobiography I try to indicate how during some of the great moments in the story of my life in a secular world, I became increasingly aware that God's hand was on me. Hence, my aim in this narrative is straightforward enough: it is to bring glory to God by coming out into the open, highlighting some of the ways He has blessed me very richly indeed, and claiming that I have been aware of His continuous presence in my life even when I have drifted away from Him and been off my guard while chasing after some worldly goal and ephemeral pleasure. Like many people through the ages, I can affirm that great indeed has been His faithfulness to me through all the years of my life and that I have never lost the sense of wonder at His "amazing grace" for me.

My background and perspective

I thought that in order to achieve my aim I should begin by bringing into my narrative a little of my background, and thus lay the ground for subsequently explaining in an unsophisticated way how I view my claim of a religious experience (and its standing). I should say that I am not accustomed to writing about my faith and that this narrative does not profess to be an academic, well-referenced, philosophical or theological treatise. Actually, I could not even attempt such writing, given that my formal studies have not been in philosophy or theology.

As a matter of fact, my undergraduate studies concentrated instead on the Physical Sciences and Mathematics, whilst my postgraduate studies were in Education — as befitted my professional career as a Secondary School teacher and later, as a Lecturer in a College of Education (at Huddersfield) which, in time, became the School of Education of the University of Huddersfield. And in the latter part of my professional life (that is, from about 1980 to 1996, when I retired from full-time employment at the university), it was Educational Research that had increasingly grabbed my interest. I had by then risen to the position of Reader and Head of the Centre for Educational Research in the University's School of Education and I had come to realise that the different styles of research in Education (and indeed in the Social Sciences generally) were grounded in various philosophical views about the nature of knowledge, about the social world and about human beings. As a result, I had become acquainted with the criticisms and misunderstandings of the scientific method and with the opposing, philosophical ideas that have influenced various models of social research (Popkewitz, 1984; Smith, 2000). This is not to say that I can claim to have a deep understanding of the concepts, principles and theories that have underpinned research and development in the Social Sciences and in the Physical Sciences. Thus, concepts like "Black holes" and "Dark energy" in cosmology, let alone "String theory" and "Membrane theory", and indeed the possibility of developing a scientific "Theory of everything", are still very difficult for me to grasp. I also find it difficult to comprehend the influential social theory of Postmodernism with its incredulity about the possibility of social progress and universal betterment through the application of reason and scientific knowledge (Lyotard, 1999; Usher *et al*, 1997).

In spite of these difficulties, what I attempted to do, as a researcher in Education, was to try and disentangle in my own mind the complexities of the conceptual framework that underpins social research. In so doing I became increasingly aware that even within the Social Sciences there was a crucial philosophical debate with regard to the very methodology of research in this field. The point was that whilst researchers in the Social Sciences might acknowledge that there does indeed exist a world of empirical social reality out there (Kirk and Miller, 1986) in the sense of "the sum total of objects and occurrences within the social cultural world" (Schultz, 1971), the issue was whether it was at all possible to obtain a reliable and valid view of that reality independently of the process and circumstances of viewing it.

It then occurred to me that this very same tantalising issue and the ways of dealing with it might be relevant to articulating the standing which I claim for my experience of the "Ultimate reality" from a Christian perspective — that is, the "reality" of an immanent and transcendent God. I therefore resolved that although I am not a sociologist or a philosopher or a theologian, what I could nevertheless do was to enquire about the approach used to tackle the above issue when investigating social reality. I then found that the issue opens up the question of what exactly is "real" in any social situation and that the methods of enquiry that this issue generates, attempt to ascertain (among other things) the reliability and validity of researchers' observations and interpretations of social reality. I therefore turned to the methods of enquiry employed by researchers in the Social Sciences in order to find out whether I could apply an appropriate method for establishing the reliability and validity of my own religious experience.

In search of a method to validate my religious experience

Clearly, there was no question of using a method of social enquiry that was based on the belief that the social world exists as an interacting system of variables that can be measured and that the relationships between these can be identified and explained. I was of the view that such a method would not prove anything — it would be rather like conducting scientific experiments in order to validate the effectiveness of prayer (Clements-Jewery, 2005). Instead, an approach to social research which seemed at first to be germane to my enquiry was that of **Phenomenology** (Husserl, 1970). My understanding was that this is the study of human experience during which one's subjective response to a particular experience as well as the issue of whether that experience is objectively "real" or not, are temporarily left out of account. "Experience" here refers to what constitutes the stream of consciousness, and a variant of this approach which seemed particularly relevant (as my interest was in a spiritual "reality" beyond myself), was **Transcendental Phenomenology** (Moustakas,1994). I thought that if one were to adopt this variant of the approach to the study of one's internal experience of being conscious of God's presence, one would engage in a disciplined and systematic effort to "bracket off", step by step, any suppositions, preconceptions, and prejudices (in connection with such an experience) that one might have from one's previous life experiences and studies, and let the phenomenon — that is, one's consciousness of God's presence in one's life — speak for itself. I also thought that if, like Heiler (1958), one conceptualises prayer as a "social phenomenon" which "displays a communion, a conversation between an *I* and a *Thou*", as in Buber's (1947) mystical philosophy, this approach would apply to the study of the phenomenon of one's awareness of, and relationship with, God in prayer. However, I realised that this approach requires too that the perspectives of other people (on their own experiences of God's presence in their own lives) be also obtained. The idea here is that this is a way of verifying one's experience, the expectation being that from one's conversations with other people would emerge a reciprocal understanding of such experiences and a correct evaluation of their "reality".

But although I found this methodology intellectually attractive, I decided not to apply it to my own enquiry. This is because I felt uncomfortable with a particular aspect of the methodology and the following account of the methodology reflects the reason for my unease even though I had no personal experience of how the methodology works in practice:

> *"one of the difficulties with phenomenology, and why phenomenologists are so hard to read, is that they try and do so many things inside their heads. They sit still in their chairs trying to do six things at once and end up disappearing into a transcendental ego which takes off into a realm of philosophical abstraction. They become unearthed from tangible sensible reality and lost in cerebral formulations. If you try and become your data, reflect on it and reflect on your reflecting on it, all inside your own head, you disappear into a mind-loop"*
> (Hawkins, 1988).

To be frank, I realised that Phenomenology was not my scene! I am very reserved by temperament and I resolved that I was not suited to validating my intense, personal, intimate experience of my encounter with God either by lengthy, agonising, and possibly morbid introspection, or by talking about it to others in a group — and attempting to establish that there is an admissible degree of coherent religious experience in the group. Also, I thought that I did not possess the necessary attributes and interpersonal skills which seemingly sharing experiences in a group requires. My stance may come as a surprise given that in my capacity as Programme Leader in a Higher Education institution for some 20 years or so (as I relate later), I had to try and understand the human feelings that were sometimes evoked during the transparent and collective process of programme validation and review (by academic peers). However, my experience of the formal (and, in my view, heavy-handed and adversarial) system of academic validation seemed to me to be irrelevant in the circumstances.

But to return to my enquiry, I realised that whilst I was not temperamentally attuned to the methodology of Phenomenology, I could nevertheless,

a) look further for a possible method of enquiry for validating my religious experience

b) draw on my insights (into the enquiry methods that I was familiar with, given my training and practical experience in Educational Research)

Pursuing further a method to validate my religious experience

My enquiry was helped by the thought that, even in the physical world, the notion of what is "real" is not so straightforward. For example, there is an argument about which is the "real" table on which I am at present writing; that is, is the table the solid object which is represented to me by my physical senses or is it "the mad whirl of electrons suggested by the scientists" (Curtis, 1965) — not to mention the other entities / "particles" which result from the interaction between the energy fields at the sub-atomic level? To sharpen this point (with regard to social reality) I found that, from the perspective of social research, probing the "realities" of a social situation is no mean task. One approach is to argue that what is "real" in a social situation is the social interaction among those who participate in the situation. Such social interaction can generate rules that aim at governing social life and can produce beneficial outcomes, such as responsible, personal morality. One important task of social research then is to seek to understand the diverse rules in society and its collective moral wisdom. From this point of view, research in the Social Sciences is not a matter of making law-like generalisations about the correlates of social behaviour and its nature. Instead, the researcher's attention is directed towards human intentions, choices, actions and communication patterns in social situations (Popkewitz, 1984). Indeed, in so-called **Critical social research** (Sapsford and Jupp, 1996), the approach is to deepen an understanding of social interactions by bringing under close scrutiny the structural inequalities in society (such as those arising from differences in social class, race and gender) and the historical development of local traditions and institutions. This approach is seen as crucially important for the interpretation of events and draws on the practice of **"Hermeneutics"** — a methodology that is well-known for its use when interpreting Biblical texts in their original settings. This methodology is adapted in social research by likening the empirical world to a text that must be read, so that, interview data, for example, are interpreted in this way in order to shed light on the experiences and events described in the interviews and to achieve meaningful understanding.

However, in the Social Science research literature, considerable dispute surrounds Hermeneutics (Gadamer, 1976; Habermas, 1988). In particular, what a "good" interpretation might be is debatable as the process of interpretation may be inordinately tied to the feelings and value judgements of the interpreter, that is, to what he/she sees through the "horizons" of his/her cultural tradition. In point of fact, there are no hard and fast rules which will guarantee a "good interpretation" in social research, in the sense that the interpretation suits the meanings that a social group gives to events and experiences (Stevenson, 2000). This perspective on researching social reality is probably rooted in the social theory of **Relativism** which, in its extreme form, may be succinctly put as "everything depends upon who you are, where you are, what you are and when you are" (Pollard, 1998). In other words, one can never get beyond one's subjective way of seeing people and things. There is no absolute truth. It is acknowledged that even the very collection of social data is problematical because researchers cannot stand over and above the social situations that they are observing and claim that in this detached position they can observe and describe reliably (that is, with minimum error) these situations for what they "really" are. The researchers' observations are likely to be theory-laden, and as already indicated, to be influenced by the values to which they are committed and which are the product of their socialisation. Indeed, these values may be expected to influence not only how the "reality" of social life is observed, in these circumstances, but also how it is analysed, discussed, constructed and reported.

Drawing on my experience of educational research

Whilst the above arguments about social research have some merit, what I retained from this brief, initial excursion into the approach of social research to the "reality" of social situations was that any validation of my religious experience would require that the events associated with it be subjected to critical scrutiny and be interpreted in the light of my historical past and of the "rules" which govern life in a Christian community; and I continued my search for an appropriate process of validation (of my personal religious experience) by drawing on my own experiences of educational research. In so doing, the method of enquiry that came to my mind was that known as **Triangulation** (Fielding, 1988; Bryman, 1988) — a term that derives from surveying and that means taking bearings from various landmarks. It is a method widely used in educational research and if it were to be applied to my enquiry it would presumably entail verifying the reality of my religious experience by comparing it with that of a number of different people giving accounts of their own spiritual experiences. I thought that this approach was justified given Hicks' (1998) suggestion that one could take one's experience of God "as a wholly reliable source of truth" and verify it with other sources of truth, beginning with the documented, genuine, religious experiences of many Christians in history — let alone the recorded experiences of so many characters in the Bible. I then went on to think that one might also tackle the theme of reliability in the sense of "synchronic reliability" (Kirk and Miller, 1986), by looking at the similarities in the religious experience of people within the same time period. The point here was that I could try and find out if my religious experience whilst living in an altogether secular world was being replicated by my contemporaries (such as those in the Lay Witness Movement within the Methodist denomination); and if the documented descriptions of our individual experiences were compared without however adopting the methodology of Phenomenologists, the extent of agreement between the descriptions could then be taken to be an indication of the reliability of my religious experience. A sequence to this way of thinking about the replication of experience was that if my own religious experiences were not isolated or occasional but were constantly repeated in my own life, they would then "hold some suggestion of self-validation", as Reid (1961) might have put it.

My approach to validating my religious experience

But important as Triangulation, Replication and Self-Validation are, I expect a key question for many people is whether one individual's religious experience can be generalised, by which they mean, I guess, whether it is possible for everyone (or at least most people) to have such a religious experience. This concept of **Generalisation**, when expressed in formal, statistical and probabilistic terms, means making inferences about a characteristic of a population (such as, its ethnicity) from a representative sample of the population using an appropriate measure of that characteristic. But interesting as such *Statistical Generalisation* is, it seemed unlikely that the validity of my religious experience could be established in this way. Also, I thought that, as far as an individual case of religious experience such as mine is concerned, more to the point was how *Generalisation* is conceptualised in *Case Study research* in the Social Sciences. The reasoning in such research is that the important criterion when one is generalising from the findings of a Case Study is their relevance to building theory (and not their statistical significance expressed in probabilistic terms) (Yin, 1984; Merriam, 1988). This perspective on Generalisation may well be seen to go against the grain but it led me to the thought that any claim that my encounter with "Ultimate reality" is a valid case of religious experience could only be justified if that experience contributed to the continuing development of theoretical propositions regarding religious experience, in general. These would provide a framework for further observations of the phenomenon of religious experience — granted that any existing relevant theoretical propositions would not be modified and/or overthrown merely by new observations but by "better" relevant theoretical propositions (Popper, 1972). Admittedly, being a Christian is not a matter of theorising about Christianity but of living a Christ-like life in practice and one may well argue that "there is no such thing as Christian theory" (Lennon, 2003) and that "everything we are discovering about Christ is for living"; nonetheless, I thought that the Case Study approach was acceptable for my purposes and it stiffened my resolve to try and articulate the "reality" of my religious experience (as I do in the next section) and to present my autobiography as a case in point of authentic religious experience. My hope, therefore, is that my brief case history will resonate with the religious experience of other Christians and will be validated in this way; and that my picture of God's intervention in my life may make some contribution to generalisations about the reality of religious experience.

The "reality" of my religious experience

I accept that my deep religious experience of how the living God, in His grace, revealed Himself to me and of how His love has penetrated to the very core of my being (thus initiating in my soul a positive response to Him) is undoubtedly beyond comprehension and explanation in terms of scientific thinking and of secular philosophy. Yet, for me, this intensely felt, altogether mysterious experience of the nearness of the Divine has been "real" in the sense that this experience provides me with ample evidence that God truly exists independently of and external to me. Of course, on its own, such evidence is not conclusive. But my conscious, intimate, continuous contact with the Divine, over some 60 years or so, through the fellowship and illumination of the Holy Spirit, is as concrete as it can be in the circumstances. This conviction is now deeply rooted in my mind — so much so that I would say that it has become for me an unquestionable "fact" of my religious life. I am well aware that this so-called "fact" is not amenable to the process of empirical falsification necessary to establish it as a scientific "fact". I am also aware that what I am affirming as "fact" can be dismissed outright on a number of grounds. It could be said, for example, that my conviction of God's presence was sheer superstition, or wishful thinking, or even that it was an "illogical belief in the occurrence of the improbable" (Stott, 1992), and was simply the product of social conditioning at home and in the church. But for me, my knowledge of God is based on the impinging presence of God, assisted by the continuous infusion of His grace, and on my knowledge of the biblical revelation of an immanent and transcendent God. However, this knowledge of a "reality" beyond the reach of scientific research has been considerably extended and enriched through an enquiring faith even whilst I became engrossed in my profession and enjoyed life to the full in a secular society. To my mind, these components of my knowledge of God hang together very well indeed — albeit, within the particular belief system founded on the central tenets of Christianity and anchored in a moment of history, some two thousand years ago (Coulson, 1966). This caveat is important for, whatever I may experience or feel or choose to believe in connection with the existence of God, the historical fact of the life of Jesus, together with the fact of his teaching, are objective and independent of me and can therefore be subjected to close scrutiny.

But I guess there is a question about how far I have been able to resolve intellectually and without compromising my faith, the conflict (at the philosophical level) between the content of my faith, with its set of internally consistent Christian beliefs (about the active presence of God in to-day's world), and the scientific view of the world, with its own set of theoretical perspectives (of "reality") that give direction to thinking in the Physical Sciences. My answer to this very pertinent question is that I am a fully integrated person. There is no inconsistency between, on the one hand, my attitude of faith and, on the other hand, my propensity for critical enquiry in matters secular and religious. I am fully conscious of the implications of claiming that I have intimations of a divine presence in my life; and I don't think that my own interpretation of my religious experience should be dismissed as nonsense or explained away as one of the archetype-like elements of the "collective unconscious" (in Jung's psychological theory).

Reflecting further on the above question, I can say that the resolution of this philosophical conflict has been achieved in my life by both acknowledging and confronting the very clear distinction between the abiding Judaeo-Christian values (such as the *"Golden Rule"* in Matthew 7:12) and the values embodied in the scientific method in the Physical Sciences (such as the commitment to empirical — analytical research). Whilst I admit to falling woefully short of expressing these Christian values in my daily life and thus selling the gospel short, I recognise the potential of these values for godly living. I have tried to make them my own by attending to the compelling love of God for me as I learned about His grace through the teachings of the Church and through experiencing the peace, comfort, joy and "blessed assurance" of the Holy Spirit as He works in my heart. This learning process was down to the family circle too, for this is where my faith came to birth, where it was nurtured, and where it grew. However, a number of other factors contributed to this growth in faith, in spite of reading about the secular world's scientific rationalism and postmodern ideas about truth. To name but some of these contributing factors, there were the overwhelming sense of the sheer mystery of existence, the vastness of the universe, the wonder at the beauty of creation, the ingenious design of the physical world, the uplifting power of some pieces of music (both religious and secular), and crucially, the forces for good in the world (as shown, for example, in the demolition of the Berlin wall and in the dismantling of the apartheid system of government in South Africa).

In the end, I think what matters is the prevailing sense of a continuous encounter with the mysterious "reality" of God in my soul. This sense is a God-given gift that I cannot refuse to accept and this autobiography is an attempt to give a brief description of this encounter at only a few, critical, points in my life. It follows from the foregoing in this section that the description has a particular theme for a focus. The theme is that God is present in us through the agency of the Holy Spirit, and intervenes in all the events of our lives — my life being a case in point. The case is organised chronologically and a large part of it relates to my professional career.

I should say that when writing my memoirs I had in mind my own children and grandchildren as my audience and that I saw my narrative as my way of telling them what the Lord has done for me. I also think that it is important for me to add that I am the one and only one responsible for the description of the events that I have included in this autobiography. As a researcher in Education I am well aware that the credibility of my life history (as I relate it in this autobiography) is an issue and I am keen not to run away from the possible criticisms that might be levelled at this descriptive account of the story of my life. Put simply, the question is: how do my readers know that I am telling "the truth"? My answer is that I was not prepared for the task of piecing together a valid and reliable account of the events that I describe and of the accompanying feelings and thoughts; and that I had not therefore kept a diary of events. However, I would claim that I have been able to remember fairly well these past events and that I have tried to describe them as accurately as I could, whilst admittedly bringing my own perspective to the descriptions. I also take the point that I have not cross-checked my observations of events with independent witnesses' accounts of the same events and that it is impossible for me to verify how representative of my eventful life my sample of events is. Regrettably, I am not in a position to circumvent these flaws in my methodology — all of which boils down to saying that I fully appreciate that I am asking my readers to take on trust what I say.

2

My childhood years in Mauritius

There is little in what I remember of my early childhood that is of direct relevance to the particular slant that I am giving to my autobiography — the slant being a consequence of my proposition that God has intervened in my life. Nevertheless, given the crucial importance of children's early relationships in the development of personality (according to Freud's psycho-analytic theory), I thought I would start with some of my childhood memories.

[1] I was born in Mauritius, in 1931, in the rural village of *Montagne Longue* (Long Mountain), at the government quarters for the local hospital's nursing personnel (of whom my father was one), and grew up there during my early childhood years. My earliest recollection of life during those years is of the occasional family trip to the settlement of *Crève-Coeur*, going through the sugar-cane plantations on both sides of the road over a distance of some three miles. We would stop on the way to visit friends of the family (one of whom I seem to remember had a large well-stocked garden) and then proceed to our destination at *Crève-Coeur* — where the Cossigny family resided. I did not appreciate then what an idyllic setting *Crève-Coeur* is. It is situ-

---

1   *The summit of the Pieter Both mountain*

ated near the foot of *Pieter Both*, a mountain named after a Dutch governor of the island in the 17th century and said to be "the most impressive of Mauritius' mountains with a huge boulder poised on its tip, seemingly about to tumble to the valley below" (Wright, 1974). The mountain was a convenient landmark for navigators before the opening of the Suez canal in 1869 — a development which brought about the decline of Mauritius as a port of call for ships going to South and East Asia.

But why go on trips to an even more remote corner of the island, one might well ask? I guess it was because a strong bond of Christian friendship had been forged between my mother and "Grandmère Cossigny" (as we used to call the widowed mother of the Cossigny family) probably through my mother's conversion from Roman Catholicism to the Seventh-Day Adventist denomination which had recently been proselytising on the island. I was too young at the time to realise (as I did later on when we visited the family, after having left *Montagne Longue*) that a deeply religious atmosphere permeated this Christian outpost. Instead, what has stayed with me about these occasional trips are mundane matters like the memory of ox-driven carts (over-loaded with sugar-canes on the stony roads to and from *Crève-Coeur* and led by men on foot), the feeling of delight at the sight of the Cossignys' seemingly large wooden family house and its extensive grounds, densely populated with a variety of tropical trees, flowering shrubs, and creepers of various kinds.

As I have already indicated, there is little in my early childhood

² years in *Montagne Longue* which seems to be of direct relevance to the theme of my autobiography. The same may be said about the later years immediately after my family's move from *Montagne Longue* to the government quarters for the medical person-

2   *The scarlet flowers of the "flamboyant" tree (also known as the "flame-tree")*

nel of the Victoria Hospital at Quatre-Bornes; and soon after that, in 1939, to our own family house at Beau-Bassin — a small town which apparently "takes its name from the pool in the Barkly Experimental Agricultural Station" (Wright, 1974). As I remember it, the station experimented with growing a variety of vegetables.

I guess my parents thought that this last move of the family would be of great benefit for their children's education because Beau-Bassin was then renowned to have one of the best Primary Schools for boys in the country, judging by the relatively high number of its pupils who won the Primary School/Junior scholarships and "exhibitions". This financial assistance was awarded by the government annually to the best under thirteen year old "competitors" (12 boys and 6 girls) in the Primary School Scholarship examination at the end of their Seventh Year at school (Benett, 1966). These scholarships and "exhibitions" provided mainly free tuition for secondary school education. This award guaranteed a place for boys at the Royal College, Curepipe (and at the College's Annexe in Port-Louis), then the only Government Secondary School for boys in the country; and, similarly, a place for girls at one of the four Loreto Convent Secondary Schools. I guess the success of the Beau-Bassin Primary school for boys was attributable (at least in part) to aggressive coaching (in the key academic subjects of English, French, Geography and Arithmetic), accompanied at times by the use of the rod!

Beau-Bassin was a satellite township well situated on the tarmac "Royal Road" from Port-Louis, the capital (on the North-West coast of the island), to Mahebourg (on the South East coast), the former main town when the French came to Mauritius. Also, Beau-Bassin was well served by the busy railway line from Port-Louis to Curepipe. Furthermore, Beau-Bassin is close to Rose Hill (another township) as well as to Port-Louis, and both Rose Hill and Port-Louis could each boast of a theatre built to European design — the Plaza theatre at Rose Hill being "the largest theatre in the Indian Ocean" with 1,300 seats (Wright, 1974). There were thus many opportunities for the local artists to offer musical concerts and recitals of French poetry. In addition, there were annually the productions in French of well-known operas and plays (by touring actors from theatre companies that came over from France). It was sheer bliss to watch, for example, the performance of Bizet's "*Carmen*" or that of Molière's *Le bourgeois Gentilhomme*. It was much later though that I began to appreciate what great opportunities these towns offered for personal development. Port-Louis, in particular, was where there were many places, objects and documents of historical, social, and political interest. To mention but a few, one would find in Port-Louis: (a) the famous letter from Queen Alexandra to the Mayor of Port-louis addressed to Mauritius, West Indies, (b) the "*Jardin de la Compagnie*" (the garden used by the employees of the French East India Company) and (c) the National History Museum which "hosts the only known complete skeleton of a single Dodo" (Wright, 1974), that "best known representative of Mauritian birdlife" (Strauss, 1993) and after which, "the largest sport club in Mauritius" was named (Lenoir and Brunel, 1974). But it was the Archives Office which endeared itself to me, if only for a short time, as I researched the history of Education in Mauritius. The office is where is to be found Charles Darwin's letter in which he speaks of the "pleasant gardens, and fine fields of sugar cane growing amidst huge blocks of lava" (Wright, 1974).

But to return to my own Primary School years at Beau-Bassin, the abiding memory of these years is one of benevolent classroom discipline with class teachers standing in front of packed multi-racial classes (with pupils sitting on benches arranged in rows) and delivering well-paced lessons. The teachers would use blackboards for explanations, occasionally posing questions to the whole class or to individual pupils in order to test knowledge and understanding. Teaching at that level was syllabus-bound with an emphasis on Spelling and Grammar in both French and English and on drill for Arithmetic. Presumably the winds of change in teaching methods had not yet blown through the education system in Mauritius so that concepts underlying the so-called "progressive, child-centred education" were probably alien to the teachers at the time. I am referring to concepts such as that of "experiential learning", in particular the idea that children need to experience "concrete operations" (Piaget, 1950) on visible and tangible objects and materials before moving on to formal, "propositional" thinking. Also, the concept of group activity in class (the idea that pupils can benefit intellectually by working co-operatively in small groups in class) did not probably appeal to teachers, given the sitting arrangements for pupils. Nevertheless, this traditional didactic method of teaching must have suited me well for I completed successfully my six years of Primary School education — the first phase of my formal education. My success enhanced greatly my self-esteem and assured me of my academic ability so that I was confident that I would pass the examination for admission to the Royal College, Curepipe (and to its Annexe at Port-Louis), and indeed this is what happened.

However, the school was by no means the only educational factor in my life during these late childhood years. As I have already indicated, my home and my Church were two other powerful educative factors. Growing up in a nuclear family I must have been learning a great deal at home (with three sisters and two brothers), particularly in response to my mother's affectionate care for all of her children. The family was indeed "the primary religious institution" for me (Morris, 1959). Importantly, my mother was a woman of faith and I guess that arising from the strong commitment to the new faith which she had embraced a few years earlier, there developed in all of us a strong sensitivity to spiritual matters. For my part, I was already beginning to get a sense of the numinous and an attitude of belief in God during these pre-adolescent years. Attending the Beau-Bassin church on the Sabbath day (Saturday), every week, with the family, (apart from my father who was most of the time at work) reinforced this growing belief, as did the regular and systematic reading of the Bible at home, the organised group activities for the young people of the church, and the annual, week-long "Rally" of members of the denomination from all over the country. The "Rally" was held at the church in Beau-Bassin. It was an event characterised by the pastoral *cum* administrative visit of a team of ministers (of the denomination) from Europe. I well remember these annual events — not only because of the large numbers who attended and of the impressive catering arrangements for hot meals and for delicacies (such as meat samosas) that were prepared in the grounds of the church (in between the conifers that thrived there), but also because of some convincing preaching. For example, on such an occasion, one popular Mauritian preacher, well known for his generally jo-vial demeanour and jokes, delivered a rousing sermon on Isaiah's penetrating question to King Hezekiah of Judah about the visit of the messengers of the King of Babylonia to his country: *"What did they (the messengers) see in the palace?"* (Isaiah 39:4). It is a question which has remained with me to this day whenever I am tempted to show off when people come to visit me at home!

3

My years of adolescence and of young adulthood

An early, heavy blow to my self-esteem came from an unexpected direction when I was on the threshold of adolescence. The punch took the form of a question addressed to me by one of my older sisters. It was about my harsh and rude behaviour towards one of our domestic "servants" who was at that time cleaning the floor of the large verandah in our family house at Beau-Bassin. The question was direct: why are you being so harsh towards this "servant"? I don't recall what I had actually said to the "servant" at the time, nor the reason for my behaviour. What I do know is that somehow that question penetrated to the very depth of my soul and made me reflect on my behaviour; for, around that time (that is, about the age of 12), I was becoming increasingly arrogant and self-assertive, and, in particular, very demanding with regard to the services that our domestic workers provided. As a matter of fact, as I realised later, such behaviour is part of my natural self. Undoubtedly, I am at heart a "slave driver" — as a colleague at work told me once when I was a House Master at the Royal College, Port-Louis! In truth, when I am in a position of authority, I find that if I allow myself to be controlled by my human nature, as St Paul might put it (see Romans 8: 1 to 8), I want to dominate, and to give orders!

Unfortunately, this innate appalling tendency in my adolescent behaviour was being reinforced by events in my life at the time. Thus, in the years immediately prior to the critical incident that I mention above, I had been doing very well at school in terms of my academic achievements. Not only had I completed my Primary School education successfully, but also, as already indicated, at the age of 11, I had passed the highly competitive examination for entry to the prestigious Royal College, Curepipe. The college provided a Grammar School type of education (with the study of Latin for all pupils in the first two years). I understand that the College has now become a "Public School" (in British parlance). In point of fact its history goes back many years — at least to the year1800 with the creation of a "Central School" (under French rule), which became subsequently the "Lyceé des Iles de France et de la Réunion" (Benett, 1966). To its credit the Royal College has over the years enabled many men from all strata of Mauritian society to get admission to Higher Education institutions abroad and subsequently they have occupied key posts in the professions (such as Medicine, Law, Engineering, and Teaching) and played an important part in public life. My recollection of my years as a pupil is admittedly adumbrated by prejudice — and age! However, it seems that the College then admitted a relatively large number of boys who (like the College teachers) were from what were then the economically privileged and educated upper classes of Mauritian society, that is, those of pure or mixed European (that is, Franco African or Franco Asian) descent — to judge by the colour of their skin!). My recollection is also that these were mostly the ones with the necessary self-confidence, prowess, and family history and tradition to take part in the many College sporting activities (which included Boxing and Soccer — but not Cricket!). They excelled particularly in athletics. They performed well too in the academic field and I was always impressed by their very good command of both French and English. Thus, the move from the Beau-Bassin Primary School for boys to the Royal College, Curepipe, on the basis of merit was undoubtedly something to be proud of — a feather in one's cap!

But there was more to my growing sense of superiority. The Royal College, Curepipe, was the very school where a year before my admission there, my elder brother (the first born in my family) had shone academically as a "laureate", by topping the list of successful candidates in the "English Scholarship" examination which was set by the University of Cambridge and could be said to be roughly equivalent to to-day's GCE 'A' level examination at Scholarship level. The significance of that feat of academic prowess was that, at the time, only two such scholarships were awarded by the Government of Mauritius for the whole country, every year, and these were then only available to the Royal College, Curepipe, pupils who scored the highest marks in total in the examination — one scholarship was for pupils on the Science side and the other for those on the Classical side and both were for boys only. The purpose of these scholarships was to enable the winners to pursue their Higher Education studies in Britain. The "English Scholarship" was thus the golden opportunity for pursuing a professional career for those who could not afford to pay for a university education abroad. So, in my first year at the college I was basking in the glow of my elder brother's academic success. Not only was that bad but I was also taking pride in the fact that I was myself doing well in my first year of secondary education as I was at the top of my class in terms of overall achievement in the academic subjects of the school curriculum.

On the other hand, a number of other experiences and events during my first years as a pupil at the Royal College, Curepipe had been having the effect of getting me to begin to come to terms with myself and think less highly of myself. To mention one typical experience, as a "badaut" (the cat-call for members of the Seventh-Day Adventist denomination after the name of its first pastor to come to Mauritius from Europe), I would occasionally be teased, though not aggressively, and I grew up with an awareness of being different from other people and therefore I felt somewhat isolated. Also, I was becoming increasingly conscious of my parentage. There was, for example, the occasion when an older boy hit me hard on the face on my way to the Beau-Bassin railway station to catch the train for school (at Curepipe). I expect the reason was that I was trying to become friendly with his sister but he did not approve, probably because of my lineage (that is, the Asian blood in me) — although he himself was of mixed race and had a brown skin too!

However, importantly, even though I can't remember exactly how, I was becoming increasingly conscious of Christ's sacrificial love for mankind and of God's redeeming grace for sinners like me — as Madame Comty, an elder of the Beau-Bassin church, explained so persuasively. Though somewhat self-effacing she conveyed the message of the gospel and its stupendous implications with conviction and clarity to the children in the "Junior Church". But, of course, there was also (as I have already indicated) my mother's continuing influence at home, through her insistence on the family's daily reading of the Bible (and the accompanying notes) in the morning with her, on her bed, even though her religious background was rather complex. She had grown up with a fervent Anglican father and a devout Roman Catholic mother and had married my father in a Roman Catholic church although he was Indian by birth.

There were other events around that time which also made a deep impression on me. One of these was the death of one of my grandfathers. I got the news of his heart attack on the way home from school and it got me to pray fervently for his recovery to good health believing that if I asked God to keep him from dying He would answer my prayer!

Other events included the deaths of two church-going young men around the same time. If my memory serves me well, both died accidentally when they touched live main electric wires: one during a cyclone which had blown down the electricity poles and left live wires lying on the ground, the other when crawling under the basement of his family house. The funeral of the former was a very emotional event indeed. Picture the scene (for the funeral) in the church: the grey-haired father, clearly well advanced in age and well-known in the church community, standing by the harmonium in front of the congregation and singing on his own, but accompanied by the music, the wonderful hymn which ran something like this:

"Does Jesus care ....?
Oh, yes, He cares
I know He cares
His heart is full with my grief..........
I know my Saviour cares"

No less moving during these adolescent years was yet another funeral! It was that of our Pastor's daughter. She was one of two children of a Swiss family who had come as missionaries to Mauritius in the 1940s during the Second World War. I think she died of diphtheria and was 12 years old. Again, picture the scene with the father himself conducting the funeral service — perhaps because no Mauritian had yet risen to the position of pastor in the denomination. Remarkably, his well-known eloquence as a preacher was unabated even at such a time as that.

It was also around that sombre time in my life that I was beginning to experience some unease with my school work. My difficulty was that I had opted for the Classical Side in my second year at the Royal College but I was beginning to find the study of Latin and of Greek (almost solely through the conjugation of verbs, grammatical declension and translation) not to my liking even though I was doing well in these subjects — to judge by my marks in the school tests.

These then were some of the experiences that troubled me during this dark period of my adolescence and which together with my sister's tantalising question about my abusive behaviour had the impact on me of wanting to repent and indeed deciding to do so. Thus it was that I began to crave for a deeper knowledge of the Christian faith and to live the life of the faithful. It would be another seven years or so though before I decided to be baptised and in this way to yield my whole life to God in response to the work of the Holy Spirit in me; and these seven or so intervening years were to be quite eventful too. A new Pastor had come soon after the end of the Second World War. He was also from Switzerland and had started a short course which was intended for the young people in the church and was on the key doctrines of the Christian Church. So, I joined the small group who attended the course. It offered a clear presentation of the key beliefs of the church. It was, in effect, building on the religious foundations which were being laid at home and was attempting to pass on something of the mystery of human life. Later, in my teens, another Pastor came from Europe too — this time from Belgium. His wife started a men's choir and I joined it along with a number of other men (young and old) from the church. Choir practice was fun. It had the effect of bonding us as a group. In addition to the choir, there were formal religious meetings and leisure activities for the young people of the church. What I enjoyed most among these were the trips to the seaside and, on occasions, camping in tents — the favourite beaches being those at *Pointe aux Sables, Gris-Gris* and *Blue Bay.* At school I had by then moved to the Science side and I was doing well. Indeed, at the end of my fourth year at the Royal College, Curepipe, I won a government "exhibition" for ranking among the best pupils in the class in terms of academic achievement. The "exhibition" entitled me to free tuition for three years.

A year later at about 16 years of age, I passed the Cambridge School Certificate examination and "qualified" for entry to the Sixth Form (also known then as the "English Scholarship class") — the term "qualified" indicating that in addition to passing the examination at "credit" level in a number of subjects, I had obtained a "credit" in English Language, the key subject for the transition to the Sixth Form. The importance of "qualifying" cannot be stressed enough, for only a small proportion of the examination candidates "qualified" every year. "Qualifying" was regarded as having reached the gold standard in education, and was a prize well worth having as it opened up a window of career opportunities for the young. However, my own success in the School Certificate examination was somewhat tainted by bewilderment for two reasons. The first was that one of my cousins who was, I thought, absolutely brilliant in English had not "qualified" that same year. Yet he was on the Classical side and his standard of English was to my mind "very high" indeed, probably helped by having been brought up in the Church of England and therefore being in contact with the English speaking clergy, among whom were British nationals (whereas our Pastors in the denomination were from francophone countries). The other reason was that I had failed in History although I was convinced that, as required, I had answered correctly five questions in the examination paper! But I am no longer puzzled about this failure now that I know something of the unreliability of examination results due to human error!

Following in the steps of my two older brothers, I progressed to the Sixth Form. By then it had changed from being called the "English Scholarship class" to becoming the two-year Higher School Certificate (HSC) class — whilst the award of the "English Scholarships" remained for the best performers in the annual external examination at this level of education. As one could stay at the College in the Sixth Form until the age of 20, I had three attempts at winning an "English Scholarship". I worked hard at the first two attempts but although I passed the examination on both occasions I did not get the "English Scholarship" and after that I lost interest in the course although I stayed at school for yet another year.

That last year in the Sixth Form in 1951 was unsettling because the lure of travelling abroad to Europe was becoming overwhelming. My mother and my younger sister had gone to England to join the second of my two brothers who was beginning his medical studies there. My parents had by then bought a house in London and my father was planning to join my mother as he was due to retire from his post at the local hospital, in Beau Bassin, in the near future. My elder sisters were bringing up their own families in Mauritius. One of my elder brothers had come back from England as a medical doctor, and had started a family with his Irish wife (who was a Roman Catholic) and a baby son.

It was also during that year that took place an event which was to change my life for ever. What happened was that the annual "Rally" at the church was particularly exciting as it hosted the meetings of the senior Pastors and administrators of the denomination who had come from Europe to the region for the "Rally" and presumably wanted an updated account of how much headway the denomination was making in Madagascar, and in the Mascarene islands of Reunion, Rodrigues and Mauritius. What I do vividly recall is that the visitors did a lot of preaching and, at the end of one of the sermons, the leader of the visiting party (an American who preached in impeccable French!) appealed for a commitment to Christ. I could no longer resist the prompting of the Holy Spirit and walked to the front in response to the appeal. I was subsequently baptised and became a member of the Beau-Bassin church. There was nothing spectacular on the outside when I got out of the waters of baptism but I well remember having such a feeling of calm and serenity. Soon after, I was made Vice-President of our small Youth Group in the church and later the local Pastor enquired whether I would like to train for the ministry in the church. However, fully conscious of my limitations, specially of my inadequate verbal fluency, I decided not to go down this road.

By then I was in my last months in the Sixth Form and unfortunately I was making friends with a couple of girls of my age and was no longer concentrating on my studies — though still hoping to win the "English scholarship"!. This was not to be, but more importantly, I was very soon to be shown my future career in a most remarkable, providential, way as I describe in the next section.

4

Side-tracked careerwise

So, I left school at the age of 20, at the end of my fourth year in the Sixth Form, and straightaway the question of getting a job surfaced. Barred from working on Saturdays on religious grounds, having no political affiliation, and no one in civil society to turn to, employment was a major problem for me. Teaching in one of the many private secondary schools that were beginning to mushroom all over the country was therefore the one possibility; and I applied for a teaching post in a few of these schools but encountered straight refusal by all except a well-known one in Rose Hill where the Principal offered me a teaching post.

However, around the same time, the Royal College, Curepipe (where about a month before I had completed my secondary school education), advertised nationally a temporary post of Assistant Teacher for Science. So, along with a few other prospective candidates (all former Royal College educated young men), I applied for the post and was interviewed along with the others but received no further information about the outcome of my application. What was therefore my utter surprise and amazement when I went to the private secondary school in Rose Hill to take my teaching post to be told by the Principal: "What are you doing here? I understand you have got the job at the Royal College, Curepipe" — the plum job in the most prestigious secondary school for boys on the island! I knew then that the hand of God was clearly in this — there is no other possible explanation for this! I say this because as a school pupil, I had not shown any sign of leadership potential waiting to be released, not having taken part in any sports and not having had any position of responsibility at the school, such as that of Prefect (like one or two of the other applicants). Thus it was that though naturally shy, retiring, and physically weak, I had been called by my heavenly Father to a career in teaching — an attractive vocation in many ways! I believe God gives us what is the very best for us according to His will.

I had a very warm welcome at the school by the "Rector", Dr. A. Constant (who had only recently arrived from Britain), and by all the staff. How could I have imagined a month or so before that I would be sitting in the imposing, well-furnished, large staff room with some who had been my teachers over the last eight years or so and indeed were renowned nationally for their intellectual calibre. But "the blessed assurance" that I was acting according to God's will for me was what made me completely relaxed and unafraid in that academic environment, as well as committed and hard-working.

I learned a lot about teaching in the six months or so that I was to stay in my post teaching Mathematics and Chemistry from Form I to Form V. I guess the enthusiasm, meticulous preparation and effort one puts into one's first public assignment is probably unsurpassed in one's career. What I mean is that I was working hard and enjoying teaching — so much so that even my simple, straightforward demonstrations of experiments in Chemistry (like the burning of a small piece of magnesium ribbon or Lavoisier's experiment about the composition of air) gave a thrill to me. I also found that experiments such as these do arouse pupils' interest in the physical world and in scientific thinking, if they are carried out in an almost theatrical way. At the same time I realised early on that there was the need to check very carefully the logicality of the pupils' thinking when they were solving problems. In Geometry, for example, one can so easily be taken-for-a-ride by a pupil's apparently logical but actually wrong solution to a problem!

I also got used, very early on, to working with colleagues and under the watchful eyes of "the boss" — in this case the benign eyes of the "Rector". I remember him standing on one occasion outside the classroom by the open window, observing me teach. I remember too being questioned in an inspector-like fashion by a Senior Education officer (another British expatriate) of the Ministry of Education, after a teaching session.

I enjoyed very much marking the pupils' work, particularly their notes of experiments and demonstrations — they were so neatly written up and were so detailed and clear. But then the pupils in two of the classes that I was teaching were the best among those in their respective cohorts at school and indeed, probably in the country. They were the top streams of Form I and of Form V, respectively. There was some fun too — some of it generated by the very composition of the classes, such as the presence of two identical twin brothers in the same class and the confusion that sometimes ensued!

But, as one might expect, in any school there were other pupils who were not so well-behaved and hardworking and respectful. Consequently, as the months passed by, I was becoming somewhat disenchanted with teaching — wanting it to run smoothly all the time. Also, I was beginning to look to a secure future, and in doing so, the lure of going to Europe or to the United States of America for further studies to degree level was very strong. There was considerable pressure to study and work abroad and many of my relations and acquaintances were going in that direction. Crucially, there was the astonishing thought (put to me by an uncle) that what I was earning monthly as a temporary Assistant Teacher in a Government Secondary school in Mauritius (albeit at the reputed Royal College, Curepipe) was the equivalent of a week's wages for washing dishes in a restaurant in England! Coupled with this alluring prospect of travelling and of studying abroad was the thought that there was nothing more permanent than a temporary post in government in Mauritius (!) and that for a permanent appointment in a teaching post in Science and/or Mathematics, a relevant university degree would sooner or later be required.

At this point in time another aspect of my character showed itself. I am by nature an impatient man. The idea of waiting for the possibility that one day, the government might offer me a scholarship (to study for a university degree abroad) was not worth contemplating — keen as I was to get on in life, as I was already 21 years old! To make matters worse, as I have already hinted, teaching was showing its ugly side, with me having at times to take a hard line in disciplining some pupils for their bad behaviour in class. There was, for example, that teenager with a sneering face and an arrogant if not combative attitude that could strain personal relationships in the classroom. So, the scene was set. I resigned from my post. How could I after having seen in a very real way the powerful hand of God in my secular life, against all odds! But I suppose such are the ways of man! Soon after I was on my way to St Andrew's University, Dundee, in Scotland, to train as a Dentist — my two brothers being in the medical profession, one already qualified as a medical Doctor (as I have already mentioned) and the other in training, also as a medical Doctor. I had earlier also toyed with the idea of becoming a Pharmacist but another uncle had advised against following this particular track. He had taken a moral stance. He had argued that chemists were only working for profit and were exploiting everybody's need for good health!

But St Andrew's University was not to be my destination. For one thing, only one person in Mauritius (amongst those to whom I had disclosed where I was going after leaving my post) knew where Dundee was situated geographically!! I don't think Golf was played in Mauritius in those days!! And when I myself looked at the map of Britain, Dundee seemed such a long way from North London where my parents had settled by then and Scotland was, I imagined, so cold! But this was not all. My parents were then advised by yet another uncle who was then in London that it was cheaper for me to stay in London as I would be staying at home. So, with the approval of the Colonial Office (which was responsible in those days for placing colonial students in British universities), I was admitted to the Northern Polytechnic (now the London Metropolitan University) to study Biology to the appropriate academic level in order to qualify for admission to the course for Dentistry in a London medical school (having already qualified for the "first MB" in Physics and Chemistry).

However, it took only two weeks for me to decide that a career in Dentistry was not for me. The mere cramming of facts (or so it seemed), and never being able to see properly under the microscope what I was told was there (presumably because of my inability to focus the lenses appropriately) and a poor memory, were all factors that contributed to my decision. In addition, the thick "smog" in the autumn of 1952 in the Caledonian Road area of London, the dark grey sky, the long rows of gloomy terraced houses, and the sight of dead leaves falling on the pavements everywhere, were in such contrast to the blue clear sky of the tropics, let alone to the inviting sandy beaches and to living in large detached houses, that I thought, the sooner I went back to Mauritius the better it would be for me. I therefore opted for a change of course, and was admitted on a London University degree course in Science combining Physics, Chemistry and Mathematics — subjects more to my liking and more in accord with my intellectual ability.

I settled down to my studies but longed to get away from the cold winter days and go back to teaching in the idyllic setting of tropical Mauritius. I regretted bitterly leaving my God-appointed place in the world. How ungrateful one can be in one's youth! How I cried during my first months in England! However, two shining spots in this gloom were the weekly church service on the Sabbath and the Sunday evening service at the New Gallery in Regent Street, in the centre of London, where an American Evangelist was preaching the powerful message of God's love for mankind and of Jesus as Redeemer. I attended regularly and prayed ceaselessly for going back to teaching in Mauritius — whilst all the time grumbling harshly at my mother about having to stay in England. Little could I know then what the future held for me in England! How limited we are as humans! But thanks be to our heavenly Father that He knows what we need.

Thanks to Him too that it would not be long before Spring would come and I would see for the first time how the daffodils and the tulips spring to life in the public parks of London and in private gardens too — and what a beautiful sight it was! The effect of such an intensely personal experience (of such beauty in Nature) on the psyche is profound — in particular, the feeling of exhilaration that springs from within oneself. I then began to make friends with young people in the Church who were not Mauritians, particularly with a small group from the continent of Europe who were working in this country after the war. Also, I had until then been visiting fairly often, at weekends, a Mauritian friend who was working in London and attended Church regularly. He was much older than I was but that did not matter. His home near Highbury was walking distance from Caledonian Road and was welcoming. He belonged to a Seventh Day Adventist family with a good educational background. His wife was French and so we were able to converse in French __ much to my liking as he was widely read and very articulate in French.

As far as my studies were concerned, it was a matter of plodding on to the end, bedevilled by colds and, importantly, by an occasional, severe pain in the hip area for which I had to stay for some time in hospital at Archway and which the hospital doctors found impossible to diagnose. It was a pain which was apparently untreatable. Notwithstanding this little difficulty, I obtained the degree of BSc. Some years later, the pain in the hip area disappeared on its own somehow.

5

Making it at last?

No sooner had I graduated in 1954 that I got a salaried post as a scientist in an industrial firm in East London. However, I soon realised what my civic status in Britain was. For, shortly after, I received a letter from the British Government about reporting for National Service, even though I was not a British national — but only a British subject and, at that point, a colonial student. The very thought of being in the armed forces sent shivers down my spine! My immediate reaction to the letter was that I simply had not got the stomach for this kind of activity — let alone the necessary physical strength. To make matters worse, I was not feeling at home working in the manufacturing industry. It was not my scene.

The alternative to enrolling in Her Majesty's Forces was to go back to Mauritius, preferably to a teaching post at the Royal College, Curepipe. I therefore prayerfully corresponded with and sought advice from a teacher (Dr Karl Noël) at the Royal College, Curepipe, who was of the same denomination and had been my private tutor for some years. Furthermore, he had been a colleague during my brief stint as a teacher at the College and, quite fortuitously, I had travelled with him and his family for the one month journey by ship to Europe. His advice was to study for the Postgraduate Certificate in Education (PGCE), as success on this course would qualify me for a teaching post as a schoolmaster. However, it was a qualification which was not offered in Mauritius. In fact, it had only recently been introduced in Mauritius. Subsequently, I applied through the Colonial Office for a place on the Postgraduate Certificate in Education course at the London

University's Institute of Education as I thought, mistakenly, that in England this course was only offered at that Institute of Education! I resigned my industrial post and, to my amazement, I was paid not only my two weeks' wages but also a month's salary under my conditions of service. This money was to be very useful indeed later!

Next I received a letter from the Colonial Office which said that I had been offered a place on the one-year Postgraduate Certificate in Education course which was offered at Southampton University — a university which I had not heard of! My spontaneous reaction was to throw the letter on the floor, dismissing its content as absurd and protesting that I could not see why I should leave London where I was by now well settled — albeit temporarily! But, as God says, "my thoughts are not your thoughts, neither are my ways your ways" (Isaiah.55 :8); and I believe that by this move, at this critical time in my life, God was settling everything for me. What I mean is that not only was He enabling me to have a professional qualification but also, as I explain later, He was leading me on to the discovery of that "good thing", as the Bible puts it, a wife (Proverbs 18:22) — and what a "good thing" it has been!

Yes, I just had to go to Southampton University. Then, one day at lunch (in the University's refectory) the Lord led the way again; for, after I had bent my head to say grace silently, on my own, as was my custom, a fellow male student at the table who was on the same course as me, asked me if I was a Christian as he had observed me saying grace. When I said that I was he invited me to join the university's Christian Union group. I then discovered that at the Glen Eyre Hall of Residence for male students where I was staying, there was a very strong Christian Union group. This cheered me no end as my friend was a leading member of the University's Christian Union. Thus it was that for the first time I made friends with Christians of other denominations and realised how strong, vibrant, their faith was whether they were Methodists, Plymouth Brethren or Baptists. We were all in Christ trying to live in accordance with His commands and His will and to make known the Good News of the gospel. There were some very committed Christians indeed in the Hall and some very powerful messages were delivered at our Christian Union meetings.

It was through the University's Christian Union group that my relationship with Evelyn Smith (who was to become my wife) grew. I had become friendly with her as we attended the same course and indeed we were in the same tutorial group. Furthermore, I had met her sometimes at the bus stop for we were in lodgings that were in the same area of the town before I moved to the Hall of Residence. Nothing could have prepared me for all this. No plan of mine could have led me to this glorious and joyful time that I had with a bunch of friends in the Hall of Residence, with the Christian Union, and with Evelyn in particular, although it was not before another three months or so that Evelyn and I entered into a closer relationship which was to lead to our marriage — at the end of the academic year, having each completed successfully our programme of study! I have such a good souvenir of our evening walks to her lodgings and of the long walk on the Isle of Wight with the Christian Union group on a particular day during the Whitsun vacation of 1955. Nothing could I have done to plan my good fortune. It was all God's doing. It just showed to me how one's own plan (such as mine about staying in London) can come to nothing, whereas if we leave it to the Lord, He is then in the driving seat and all we need to do is to "trust and obey" — there is indeed no other way! The great thing is that one has then this "blessed assurance" that one is doing His will and that one is on the right path. How true it is that "in all things" God does indeed "work for good" with those "whom He has called according to his purpose (Romans 8:28).

At the end of our PGCE course Evelyn and I returned to our respective homes in Haywards Heath (East Sussex) and in London. For me the question of doing National Service in Britain came up again and I decided to go back to Mauritius. This is when I asked Evelyn to marry me. She accepted and arrangements were made by our respective families for the wedding ceremony. This took place in a church in Brighton and after the church service all the guests had a meal with us at the former King Alfred Restaurant, at Hove, near Brighton. My salary from the previous year's employment contributed towards funding our honeymoon in a Sussex village in the countryside. Our honeymoon was sheer bliss. We were now in "another world" bound as we were in the common faith

[3] that the Lord was with us and that we were doing His will for us. It was a huge leap in the dark to get married without either of us having a job! It was again a matter of "trust and obey" — there is no other way!

However, the honeymoon period soon came to an end and the reality of life together forced itself on us. We had to make up our minds about our future together and the decision was for me to go back to Mauritius on my own and for Evelyn to join me later. Thus it was that due to my parents' generosity yet again, my passage on a ship (the Kenilworth Castle) was booked and I went back to Mauritius — though not before spending a day or two at St Margaret's bay (near Dover) with Evelyn, as she had accompanied me to the harbour. We stayed at an excellent hotel all paid for by the ship's agents because the ship's departure had been delayed!

The return journey to Mauritius along the West coast of Africa was in sharp contrast to the outward journey a few years earlier along the East coast of the continent. It was the contrast in the quality of life on board two very different ships: one was a French passenger boat carrying mostly whole families from Mauritius, Reunion and Madagascar, respectively, to France, and the other was a British cargo boat carrying only a small group of some six or so Mauritian nationals and three British nationals (apart from the crew). However, the presence of the two different nationalities on board the cargo boat was to expose to me the ugly face of the apartheid regime that prevailed in South Africa at the time; for, whilst on board the ship, we (the Mauritians) sat at the ship Captain's table and had our meals with all the ship's naval officers, when we docked at Port Elizabeth (in South Africa) and went

3   *Evelyn and I on our wedding day, 20ᵗʰ July, 1955*

ashore to post our letters, we discovered that there were two separate queues at the Post Office (one for Europeans and the other for Non- Europeans) and that where you sat on a double-decker bus (that is, whether upstairs or downstairs) depended on the colour of your skin!!

Finally I arrived in Port-Louis after some four weeks or so and after having had to transfer to another cargo boat at the port of Beira (in Mozambique) in order to arrive in time for getting a teaching post and starting to teach at the beginning of the school term, at the Royal College, in September 1955. But it was not to be; I was too late. So I had to look for a job elsewhere and after three days of being unemployed — the only time I would be unemployed in my whole career! — I was offered the post of Head of Science at Bhujoharry College, one of the largest privately owned secondary schools in the country. The school was in Port-Louis and I was offered a salary commensurate with the salary for teachers at the Royal College. The significance of my appointment was that, by then, the "English Scholarships" were opened to Sixth Form pupils at private secondary schools too, and Bhujoharry College was wanting to compete with other private secondary schools and with the government-aided secondary schools (mainly, the Saint Esprit College and the Saint Joseph College) for these scholarships. The school needed a graduate Science teacher and I had arrived at the school just on time — another coincidence? The school gave me some invaluable experience of and insight into the continuous struggle for resources in Education and made me appreciate that academic achievements are possible even under relatively unsatisfactory conditions for learning.

However, one important consideration was that although my salary at that school was good compared to the initial salary for graduate teachers who worked at the Royal College as government employees, there was no scope for career progression, no official pensions scheme and, crucially, no statutory overseas leave every four years or so (which could be so convenient for further studies and for our young family) — that is, none of the benefits to which the employees in Government service were entitled. But the Lord was looking after us. He would provide a golden opportunity for me to get back into Government service and work under these very attractive conditions. Briefly, just about a year later, I was invited to apply for a post of Science Master at the Royal College, Port-Louis — which, as I have already indicated, had started as an annexe to the Royal College, Curepipe, but had by then expanded exponentially and become another Government secondary school for boys in its own right. The same conditions of service that were in force for teachers at the Royal College, Curepipe, applied to teachers at the Royal College, Port-Louis and, consequently, I accepted the invitation and started work at the College.

Evelyn too had been blessed in her professional career with her full-time appointment some months earlier as Head of Mathematics in the newly launched Queen Elizabeth College — the country's first Government Grammar school for girls. At the same time she was pregnant with our first child; and, as always, the Lord was looking after us, for a British midwife (who was the wife of our family doctor) ensured the safe delivery of our first baby son, Ivan.

The next four years or so were to be intensely occupied with bringing up our family of three children (Peter and Heather having been born soon after Ivan) and with moving house twice before settling down in Beau-Bassin, in one of my parents' houses. Evelyn managed to communicate fairly well in the local vernacular — Créole, a "vibrant" language which "derives from French" (Strauss, 1993). I think she could understand some of the preaching in French at the church which we attended. She also coped remarkably well with the domestic chores, with the help of the nannies and the cook. I expect only those who have been away from home and so thoroughly uprooted can understand what Evelyn must have been through — yet she was, I think, so very happy, being completely devoted to our young family as well as committed to her full-time work. What a blessing to have such a person as wife! Thank you, heavenly Father.

We were very happy indeed and were settling down well in Mauritius except for the fact that my appointment as Education Officer (the official title for the post of school master/mistress in Government) was still not officially confirmed after some four years or so, in spite of my recognised success with getting my pupils through their GCE 'O' level examinations and in assisting with the supervision of GCE 'A' level students attending evening classes at the Royal College, Port-Louis. However, our God intervenes in His own time — not earlier than is necessary! And after some four years or so of labouring under this cloud of uncertainty (about my appointment as Education Officer) I was finally confirmed in the post. The next stage in my career and in our family life was suddenly to unfold in a quite unexpected way and the next section describes the momentous intervention of God in my life — yet again.

6

Back to the ivory tower in England

As a matter of fact, my appointment as Education Officer came just in time for me to apply for a Commonwealth Scholarship for teachers in 1960, for it was the very year when, for the first time, this scholarship scheme was launched for the Commonwealth countries; and in Mauritius I was about the only one eligible for such a scholarship for Science teaching because of my professional qualifications. Was this another coincidence? I don't think so. I believe God's hand was again at work in my life in a very concrete way. For this scholarship was going to enable me to pursue my study of Education as an academic subject whilst giving Evelyn the opportunity to be back in Haywards Heath with her parents. In the event I was one of the two Science graduates from Mauritius who were granted the one-year scholarship and given a place on the Commonwealth Teachers' Certificate course at the University of Hull. However, the city of Hull is a long way from Haywards Heath and it was thought best for Evelyn and the children to stay with her parents in the South of England whilst I ventured to Hull, in the North of England. This arrangement did mean that for a whole academic year Evelyn would be looking after three small children whilst pregnant with a fourth and not having any domestic help! However, we knew we just had to follow God's lead. As always Evelyn coped very well indeed.

As for me, I enjoyed yet again the friendship of the Christians in the men's Hall of Residence where I was staying. It was Needler Hall, at Cottingham. I became even more convinced of the reality of the cross being at the centre of our Christian faith — the straightforward fact that Christ died for us to redeem us. This is the platform for the "Good News" — not the keeping of the Sabbath or the return of Jesus to this earth (as the Seventh-Day Adventists would so earnestly hold). Far more important is the constant proclamation of the central tenets of Christianity such as the one to be found in John 3:16 :

> *"For God so loved the world that He gave His only begotten Son, that whosoever believeth in Him, should not perish but have everlasting life."*

The words of St Paul too come sharply to mind:

a) *"For Christ has brought the Law to an end, so that every-one who believes is put right with God" (Romans 10: 4)*

b) *"So let no one make rules about what you eat or drink or about holy days or the New Moon Festival or the Sab-bath,..........the reality is Christ" (Colossians 2:16)*

c) *"For it is by God's grace that you have been saved through faith. It is not the result of your own efforts, but God's gift so that no one can boast about it" (Ephesians 2: 8-9)*

Actually, even in Mauritius I had been interested in the very clear and powerful Christmas messages of the Anglican and Roman Catholic clergy alike and had found that this same "good news" was at the heart of their messages. It is unfortunate that the rituals and traditions of some denominations of the Christian Church can sometimes cloud this "good news" — the very bed-rock of Christianity. But I recognise that the presentation of the Christian message is a real conundrum for the Church. For example, I remember being appalled during my brief stay in Madras in the 1970s (working on an educational research project) to see people queuing to kiss the glass cover of a box in which a statue of the Virgin Mary had been placed. Yet, I was later to reflect that although such acts of worship could probably be said to be bordering on idolatry, they may have been necessary in some countries. For example, when striving to explain the meanings of the sacraments in Christianity (such as those in connection with the Lord's Supper) to those who were illiterate and/or whose mother tongue was not that of the Christian missionaries who brought the gospel to them, the latter may have had to communicate their faith through imagery and symbolic physical acts although they themselves believed that God is a Spirit and that those who worship Him must worship Him in spirit and in truth (John 4:24). Anyway, over the years, I found myself being drawn more and more to the Evangelical branch of the Church because of its adherence to the basic tenets of the Church, unadulterated by other doctrines, traditions and rituals. Etymologically, as Hicks (1998) points out, the word "evangelical" refers to "those who announce good news" and the "good news is, of course, the gospel of Jesus Christ".

On the professional side, my course at the University of Hull had given me time to read about Science Education and indeed about Education, in general. Importantly, as I explain later, it had motivated me to study for a further qualification in Education, namely, the London University's Advanced Diploma in Education. But whilst I was benefiting in this way, Evelyn was having to cope with three toddlers (Ivan, Peter, Heather) and indeed with more; for she was expecting our fourth child (Sheila) who arrived whilst I was in my third term at the University of Hull. We were very grateful to Evelyn's parents for kindly helping in so many ways, and Evelyn and I triumphed over the numerous practical difficulties that we faced then. We thank God for looking after all of us during those trying times.

Shortly after the end of the 1960/61 academic year, we returned as a family to Mauritius and both Evelyn and I resumed our teaching positions as Education Officers. The years that followed brought us a lot of joy with the children as they were growing up. However, it would not be too long before we would be back in England (in 1965) because, as Government Officers, we were due for overseas leave every four years or so.

7

Back home again in Mauritius

Back in Mauritius, I had the additional responsibility of being a House Master at the Royal College, Port Louis, and was thus, again, among the chosen few given a leadership role at the school for there were only four House Masters at the school. For her part, Evelyn continued as Head of Mathematics at Queen Elizabeth College (for girls). She was as hard working as ever and was well after a brief period of illness which, in point of fact, kept us together at the foot of the Cross, utterly relying on God's "amazing grace".

At week-ends we would often go as a family to the nearby sandy beaches (such as *Pointe aux Sables* or *Flic-en-Flacq*) and to the *Pleasure Ground* (in a suburb of Port Louis), and we would socially meet with a few of the English-speaking married couples (mostly of Mauritian men married to British women). We also began to attend occasionally the Presbyterian Church in Phoenix on Sundays, as the preaching there was in English. The Minister of the church was a Scotsman. We were settling down very well indeed in Mauritius and to all accounts we had a bright future there.

I continued to enjoy the reassurance of the Lord's presence in my life and on one occasion it came in a very convincing way. As I recall it, although by then I had had experience of teaching Science in school laboratories for some seven years or so, I regret to say that I had never bothered about the fire hazards which Chemistry laboratories posed during practical chemistry sessions. One can be so self-confident as a young teacher!! However, one night I dreamed that there could be a fire in the Chemistry Laboratory and I realised that I did not know how to put it out. So, the next morning, as soon as I came to work, I rushed towards the fire extinguisher in the laboratory and asked the laboratory technician if he knew how to use it. He did not know either! So together we read the instructions. Not long after (on that same day) a group of Sixth Form boys were starting an experiment which involved dropping alcohol from a thistle funnel into a flask which was being heated on a Bunsen burner. Soon, some drops of alcohol began to run down the side of the flask and caught fire. Within seconds the laborotary technician and I leapt to the scene and put the fire out — covering the whole equipment with a thick white foam! Just imagine if we had not rehearsed how to use the fire extinguisher earlier that day! The words that ring in my ears are: "Halleluiah! What a Saviour!" Of course, such an experience may be dismissed by some people as mere prescience and by others as a chance event, but it is this continuous, occurrence of so many "coincidences" that I submit is compelling confirmation of the Holy Spirit's presence in my life. Where do dreams and ideas come from is a question which I guess many learned people have tried to answer. All I know is that the prompting of the Holy Spirit has been very real for me through all my years of consciously living under His banner.

Nonetheless, with Evelyn and me living a life of relative affluence in a Third World country like Mauritius, came the idea of building our own house with all the modern gadgetry and in a better (that is, up-market) neighbourhood. I well remember being taken on one occasion to a newly developed, private building site (near Coromandel, on the main road between Port-Louis and Beau-Bassin) with this idea in mind. I remember standing with one of my brothers-in-law at the top of the hill at the site, under a cloudless, blue sky, and looking down at the deep blue sea below asking myself "is this it? Is that all there is to living here on a small island, far from the rest of the world, and with limited access to the world of learning and to developments in the field of Education? How boring!" As a "reflective practitioner", I found myself being driven in two opposite directions by two conflicting forces: on the one hand, I could rest on our achievements so far and enjoy life in Mauritius — a life which, as we discovered later (as Mauritius became one of the holiday resorts much sought after by tourists!) was the envy of some people. On the other hand, I felt under an obligation to attend to the demands of my calling by pursuing still further my academic study of Education, and obtaining the prestigious Master's degree in Education with a view to getting a deeper understanding of Education and to rising to a higher position in the Education System locally, in the fullness of time. In the event, I started working towards satisfying both desiderata concurrently.

Thus it was that I sat the examination for London University's Advanced Diploma in Education, as an external student in Mauritius and passed. It was probably the first time that a teacher in Mauritius had taken that particular examination. Having obtained that Diploma, I next registered for the London University's MA degree in Education (by research) as an external student. Again, I knew that it was clearly the direction in which the Lord was leading me because in order to register for the degree, the University's regulations required that there had to be an Educationist locally who was appropriately qualified to supervise my research. The recommended research area was to be the school curriculum and the research topic was to be the Primary Schools curriculum in Mauritius. As it happened, around that time a UK-based UNESCO consultant had taken up his post at the local Teacher-Training College and he accepted to take on the role of supervisor for my research project. Another coincidence?

At the same time my responsibilities as a school master at the Royal College, Port-Louis, were made the more interesting when a few innovative ideas came to the fore for the House of which I was in charge. One of these was my idea of taking a group of Sixth Form boys for a trip to the neighbouring island of Reunion which, under the French system of governance, is an administrative Overseas Department of France (*Département Français d'Outre-Mer*) with representation in the French National Assembly. The trip took some organisation but the conducted tour of the island, including trekking in the high mountains at the interior of the island, was completely in the hands of the government of Reunion, so that we were led throughout by a team drawn from the special French force known as the *Compagnie Républicaine de Sécurité (CRS).*

The team organised all the necessary residential accommodation for us and provided us with all the equipment that we needed for travelling in such a mountainous island in the tropics.

To my delight, another salient novel idea came from the boys themselves. Most enthusiastically, they launched a school journal and organised its publication on strictly business lines. The production team was made up of boys from diverse socio-economic, cultural, racial, and religious backgrounds, — such diversity being a characteristic of the population of Mauritius. The journal was a multi-cultural achievement. So much for all the apparent fuss in England about multi-culturalism!

However, change and innovation were in the air not only at school but also on the domestic front. For, at the same time that these developments were taking place, Evelyn and I decided to purchase a plot of land at Quatre-Bornes, a small leafy town where many of the well-to-do particularly among the professional class lived, and where as a child I had attended the local primary school. Work on designing and building our house started in earnest. We planned to make this our home for good, with the prospect of going to England for our statutory overseas leave every four years or so. Indeed, as already mentioned, we were due for such leave in August 1965.

I can't recall any relevant spectacular intervention of our heavenly Father in our lives in the years immediately prior to our leave. However, one object lesson which I learnt from my personal, direct involvement in the building of our house has stayed with me. The point of the lesson emerged in the following way. The building of the house was progressing well until one morning just before I was going to leave home for work, the Clerk of Works took delivery of a lorry load of medium-sized stones. They were intended for the construction of a fashionable multi-coloured wall for the front of the house. But to my astonishment they all appeared to be very ordinary stones, greyish in colour. They were not, I thought, the stones (of different colours) that I was expecting and that it was fashionable at the time to use in the construction of outside walls for private houses. I panicked. I protested to the Clerk of Works that the building contractor was fooling us, but he assured me that the stones were indeed the very stones that we needed. I phoned our young architect and he too assured me that the stones were the right ones. The mason told me the same story: these stones were indeed just ordinary ones picked from the sugar cane fields but they were the right ones! I still could not believe my eyes.

[4] However, as the mason began slowly, but expertly, to build the wall, I could see a beautiful, multi-coloured, wall rising slowly from the ground. How foolish I had been! These apparently useless, unimpressive stones which I had wanted to reject were the very ones that the mason was now using and that were giving us such joy. The lesson for me was clear: it was the realisation that although one may feel that one is living an utterly useless life from the perspective of the secular world, yet the divine architect may be slowly but surely shaping this life into a productive and glorious one. Moreover, this brief encounter with the builders reminded me that "the stone which the builders rejected as worthless turned out to be the most important of all" (Ps118:22)!

But in spite of the very considerable excitement of being actively involved in building our own house, my research for the Master's degree thesis kept pulling me in an altogether different direction. Consequently, I plodded on resolutely with the empirical part of my research. This consisted in making observations of classroom situations as they occurred in a sample of primary schools, and I kept substantive notes of my observations (Benett, 1966). I also worked with equal steadfastness at the national Archives Office (in Port-Louis) on another part of my MA thesis — a brief history of the evolution of Education in Mauritius during the French occupation of the island until 1810, and during the period of British colonisation up to the early 1960s.

All of this adds up to saying that it was a very busy and exciting time indeed. My plan was to do as much as possible of the data analysis and of the report writing for the research during my three

4   *My family in 2004, at our former home in Quatre-Bornes*

months or so of statutory leave in England, that is, during the one month that we would be on board of the ship that would take us to England via the East coast of Africa, the Suez canal and France and during the two months or so that would follow. And indeed this is what happened: I surrounded myself in our family cabin on the ship with the copious field-notes that I had made in Mauritius, in the school classrooms, and proceeded with the task in hand of analysing the data.

5

5   *Our house at Quatre-Bornes, soon after its construction in 1965*

8

The moment of truth

I continued working on my MA thesis assiduously at the home of Evelyn's parents where we were staying as a family. However, it soon dawned on me that I needed more time to complete my thesis and, crucially, that the future for Evelyn and me in Mauritius could after all be precarious. Admittedly, there were prospects in Mauritius that could be very satisfying professionally for both of us. For one thing, Evelyn would have the opportunity to apply for and, God willing, get a more senior post at the Queen Elizabeth College. For another, as I would be almost the only one in Mauritius at the time who held a Master's degree in Education, I could legitimately aspire to a senior position in the Education system, or to a lecturing post in the Institute of Education which the Government was planning to set up.

Against such expectations, however, there was the worrying thought that the prospect of full-time employment for the younger generation in Mauritius was bleak: I had even seen, on one occasion, a young boy scavenging in our dustbin! On the political scene, Independence for the island was on the cards and the expectation was that it would soon be granted. Yet, the prospect of Independence for the island was not so enticing with a population approaching one million and growing at the rate of some 2 per cent, per annum (Lenoir and Brunel, 1974), with the lack of jobs, with the reliance on sugar production as the main industrial base for the economy, and with a society stratified along ethnic, class, and religious lines. In point of fact, even before I had taken my study leave, emigration to Australia, Great Britain and France, respectively, was being talked about (among colleagues and in the country generally) in view of the forthcoming Independence. This almost panicky reaction to the prospect of Independence was not without some justification. Thus, we now know that by 1971, that is, three years after Independence, unemployment had averaged 20 per cent (Gulhati,1990) — although, to the credit of the government of Mauritius that figure was brought down to 4 per cent by 1987 through a number of policy planks, such as the policy of providing preferential credit to foreign and domestic investors who specialised in exporting and the policy of attempting to attract "high-class" tourists from Europe and South Africa.

But at the back of my mind was also another worry which was that the largest ethnic group was made up of Hindus and Muslims (and accounted for some 68 per cent of the population). There could therefore be a gradual and subtle influence on religious thinking in an independent Mauritius (let alone the overt persecution of Christians). For example, there was the possibility that the notion of "pluralism" (that is, the acceptance of diverse worldviews as equally valid) might become attractive and indeed, prevail as a common-sense view of what the religious scene should be like in a multi-faith society. However, on this point, my stance was clear: "salvation is to be found through Him (Jesus) alone; in all the world there is no one else whom God has given who can save us" (Acts 4:12). I fully agree with Stott (1992) that "we Christians cannot surrender either the finality or the uniqueness of Jesus Christ"; for, central to Christianity are the words of Jesus "I am the way, and the truth and the life; no one comes to the Father, but by me" (John 14:6), granted that, as Anderson (1984) explains, the thrust of verses such as this might be that no-one can come to know God *as Father* except through Christ the Son, rather than that no one can come to know God at all except through Him. Admittedly, I have little knowledge of the non-Christian religions of the world but I had always found some of their rites (as practised publicly in Mauritius) quite unnerving. There was, for example, the masochistic mortification of the flesh at the Tamil festivals of Cavadee, when devotees would thread long needles through the flesh of their own bodies — not to mention fire-walking (when devotees walk on glowing charcoal spread in a pit)!

Yet another key consideration about whether to stay in Mauritius or not was that in some ten years or so university education abroad for our four children (as prospective overseas students in England) would be a very heavy financial burden (although we did not know then what their career aspirations would be). In the event three of them chose to study medicine and one to pursue her studies at PhD level.

In view of all these considerations, Evelyn and I began to think that although we would lose some 10 years of pensionable service in Mauritius if we resigned from our permanent posts as Education Officers, the loss would be amply compensated in the long run, given the many advantages of working and living in England. Then, with due regard to our conditions of service in government, we applied for an extended leave (without pay) from our respective posts in Mauritius and we bought a house in Haywards Heath. At the same time, I scrutinised the list of school teaching vacancies advertised weekly in the *Times Educational Supplement,* and I applied for a number of relevant teaching posts. I finally got one at the Woodside Park School (near Finchley, in London). It was a Roman Catholic Grammar school for boys. There I was, a Non-Conformist/Protestant Christian who in his childhood had often heard that the "beast" in the Bible's book *Revelation* represented the Roman Catholic Church, but had now taken a teaching post in a Roman Catholic school! Some people might see this as walking into the lions' den whilst others would see it as turning to the light (to use Plato's metaphor)! I saw it as an accommodation of my belief system called for by the particular situation in which I found myself. I spent two good years at the school teaching Chemistry up to the Oxford GCE 'A' level and Scholarship level, respectively. My work routine was to take the 6:45 a.m. train from Haywards Heath to London Bridge and then the London Underground to Woodside Park (near Finchley) — altogether a journey of some 1½ hours.

Both the academic staff and the support staff of the school were very welcoming indeed and the boys were on the whole quite receptive. I could have stayed there but for the fact that, as I believe, the Lord in His plan for me was taking me elsewhere; for, by the end of the two years I had completed my thesis and obtained the degree of MA in Education and I had resigned from my post in Mauritius. Evelyn too had given up her teaching career in Mauritius. Then, in almost unbelievable circumstances I got a post as Lecturer at the Huddersfield College of Education (Technical) in January 1968 and within four years or so I had risen to the position of Principal Lecturer in that institution. All of that happened by mere chance? I don't think so!

9

Life on the edge in the teacher-training field

How did it happen? It is again the wonderful way in which our God leads each of us according to His gracious will for our lives.

In brief, the school in London (where I was working) was having a general inspection by Her Majesty's Inspectorate for schools at one point during the time that I was teaching there. On one occasion, one of the inspectors had observed me teaching for a whole period. At the end of that period and after the pupils had left the classroom, he took me to one side and talked to me about my teaching. He then asked me if I had given any thought to moving on professionally to a lectureship in the Teacher-Training sector. It was just the clue that I needed for the direction to take for my next move career-wise. So, I applied for one of the lecturing posts that the Huddersfield College of Education (Technical) was then advertising. The College was expanding its In-service provision for Initial Teacher-Training (Technical) and therefore needed to increase its staff establishment. I was interviewed for one of the posts and appointed as "Lecturer" at the College. I took my post in January 1968.

I considered it a real privilege to be working in what was then one of only four Colleges of Education (Technical) in England. At the time, the college offered only a basic programme of Initial Teacher-Training (by both Pre-service and In-service modes) for Lecturers in Technical or Commercial subjects or in the Humanities, who worked or intended to work in the Post-compulsory sector of education, that is, mainly in Further Education colleges or in Technical Colleges. It goes without saying that these In-service trainees were all qualified specialists who brought with them a store of experience in specific fields, crafts or occupations with recognised further education credentials. Many among them were university graduates. Their lecturing responsibilities in their home institutions would consist mostly in teaching in Engineering workshops, Science laboratories and other specialist accommodations that were not conventional classrooms (such as a foundry or a computing environment). Also, at the time, the Huddersfield College of Education (Technical) staff who "lectured" on the In-Service programme were categorised either as "Special Method Tutors" or as "Education Tutors", thus highlighting the distinction between the two key elements of the curriculum for Initial Teacher-Training, namely, (a) the Special Methods of teaching various specialisms, and (b) Educational Theory (mainly, the Philosophy, Psychology and Sociology of Education, the Curriculum, and the Administration and organisation of the Education system). The "Special Method Tutors" were in far greater number than the "Education Tutors", as the former were responsible for the training of teachers in a large number of subject areas (such as Engineering, Construction, Business, Food and Fashion, Computing, General Studies and Modern Languages), whereas the latter focussed on the subject of Education. I was put with the small group of Education Tutors and from that moment on, I realised that I would be on the edge of the College academic community, particularly as the College's Day-Release, In-Service provision was initially on a small scale (because the catchment area was local) and in its infancy — whereas the Pre-Service course recruited full-time students nationally and had been established some 20 years earlier. On the other hand, the In-Service provision was the area of the College's work that was expanding. Indeed, the College began to set-up outposts all along the East coast of England from Durham to Ipswich so that, within three months or so, I was promoted to the position of Senior Lecturer and given the leadership role in developing the curriculum for the Psychology of Education for In-Service teachers.

This career path was suiting me very well. I was convinced that it was the work that the Lord wanted me to do and the whole atmosphere of the College was congenial for such work. Although I was clearly accountable to my employing organisation for my work, I enjoyed considerable autonomy of action. It was such a privilege for me to immerse myself in the Education literature freely available at the College. I therefore read a lot and also I began to write on certain concepts and theories in Education (such as the objectives-based curricula and Piaget's theory of intellectual development) that were gaining ground in the world of training and education generally, and which I thought needed explanation — hence my article, in 1969, on *"The range of goals and objectives in Industrial Training and Further Education"* in the British Journal *The Vocational Aspect of Education,* and my booklet on *An introduction to learning and teaching with particular reference to the sixteen to nineteen age range* (Benett and Grant, 1972).

Once in Huddersfield, Evelyn applied for, and got a temporary lectureship in the Department of Mathematics at the Huddersfield College of Technology (later Huddersfield Polytechnic). Subsequently she was appointed full-time in the post and on a permanent basis — against all the odds, for in those days it was difficult for married women to obtain permanent employment. In point of fact, she was the first married woman to be offered a permanent post at the College. Was this also mere coincidence? She took this golden opportunity to pursue her studies, part-time, at Master's degree level, at the University of Sheffield and specialised in Statistics. She soon earned her promotion to Senior Lecturer level; and by the time she retired from full-time employment, in 1989, she had completed 20 years of continuous, successful work in higher education. She was then free to lecture, part-time, at the University of Manchester.

Continuing with the account of my professional life, my interest in teacher education received a further impetus when more responsibilities came my way, after some four years or so, as Senior Lecturer working in the area of Initial In-Service Teacher-Training. What happened was that the post of Tutor for the University of Leeds Diploma in Further Education course became vacant. The College had only recently started to offer this advanced course at Huddersfield, under the aegis of the University of Leeds, and the position of Course Tutor was at Principal Lecturer level. I was encouraged to apply and indeed I was the internal candidate for the post probably because at the time I was the only lecturer at the college who possessed a Master's degree in Education. There were two external candidates but I got the job and I stayed in this post for the next 15 years or so. Yes, unassuming as I was, the Lord had chosen me to lead a team of colleagues some of whom were of the same status as myself (as Principal lecturers in their own disciplines). With their co-operation I developed the Course and offered it at the College and in a number of centres along the East Coast of England, with attendance on the course being in three possible modes (the Full-Time mode, the Sandwich mode and the Day-Release mode) . My experience was to be valuable later, when the College merged with Huddersfield Polytechnic and I had to launch a B.Ed degree and an M.Ed degree through all the complexities and ramifications of Quality Assurance for a CNAA degree course! God's "amazing grace" ensured that I never had any difficulty in obtaining the co-operation of colleagues for these responsibilities. What I did not know then was that the Lord was preparing me for an even more daunting task: that of taking the lead in Educational Research at the College after its designation as a School of Education when it merged with Huddersfield Poly-technic in 1974. Admittedly, although all these developments on the Post Initial Teacher-Training scene were generally acknowl-edged to be of critical importance for the image of the College in a competitive, Education market, I rather think that they were seen as marginal by most colleagues, so that for my part, life remained on the edge but was as challenging as ever.

I was also to learn how not to rely on others when fighting one's corner, however friendly they may be — but only on our God. The gist of the story is that although the Diploma in Fur-ther Education of Leeds University was an Advanced In-Service Course in Educational theory and practice for academic staff (in the Post-Compulsory Education sector) who had normally al-ready obtained a Certificate in Education together with a degree in an academic discipline or a vocational qualification, there was some uncertainty about its status because of the ambiguity of the term Diploma in the British education system. The implication for the salaries of those who lectured on the Diploma course was considerable. The bone of contention was that when Colleges of Education merged with Polytechnics, differences became apparent between the Pelham salary scale for the College staff and the Burnham salary scale for the Polytechnic staff. The important difference for me was that there was a "Bar" in the salary scale for Principal Lecturers on the Burnham salary scale, the crossing of which depended on the level of work. As the Course Leader, I had to make the case that the status of the Leeds Diploma was that of an Advanced course in Education, that is, one that was above the level of the basic, Initial Teacher-Training course, as that higher level of work would take the salaries of the Diploma course staff above the "Bar". I found myself having to fight the case almost alone because for various reasons some colleagues in the Course team and others in the National Association of Teachers in Further and Higher Education would not give me the necessary support. But, as always, I felt God's hand steering me through the muddy waters of institutional politics. To begin with, my Head of Department at the time was himself a holder of an Advanced Diploma in Education, and he was therefore willing to press for an enquiry at the institutional level into the status of the Diploma. As a result, the institution asked for concrete evidence that the level of the course was equivalent to that of similar courses in a number of other well-known universities in England. At this point, I knew that the Lord was definitely with me in this particular struggle, for it was no coincidence that my former Personal Tutor at the University of Hull had by then risen to the position of Director of the Institute of Education at that university and consequently I was able to visit him and explain my predicament. Thus began my round of visits to a few universities in the region in order to obtain the necessary documentary evidence about the contents of their own Advanced Diploma courses in Education. I was pleased to report that these universities were only too willing to certify that the status of the Leeds University Diploma in Further Education was indeed that of an Advanced course in Education. My "battle" with the Polytechnic authorities was won, and I thanked God for that!

10

Reaching new heights

The leadership of the Advanced Diploma in Further Education course had given me a taste for supervising dissertations of some 20,000 words as these were a key component of the course. I did not realise then that such supervision would prepare me for my responsibilities later on, as Reader, when I had to supervise re-search degree theses at M.Phil and PhD levels. What I did realise though was that, as Course Leader of such an important Diploma, I needed to pursue my studies in Education still further and in 1973 the opportunity to do so came. The circumstances in which the opportunity occurred were these. One morning I happened to be walking past the staircase which starts from the main foyer on the ground floor of the Administration Block of the College (at the Holy Bank Road campus) when the Director of the College was coming down the stairs and hailed me with an invitation to accom-pany him to his office nearby, as he had something to tell me. So we went together to his office and on the way he asked me whether I would be interested in a British Government sponsored project (covering the whole of South India) which centred on an evalua-tion of a newly developed curriculum for Engineering technicians in that part of the world. Of course, I was interested! This was my very first opportunity as Education Consultant and it opened for me the door to evaluation research in Education. Crucially, I was aware that such a project could lead to the degree of PhD as the scope of work was wide and the statistical data which it would generate could be explored in depth. I therefore registered with the Open University for the degree of PhD (Education) as a Part-Time student. I completed my thesis successfully in 1978. Was all this another mere coincidence? No! I believe it was God who, in His own way, was behind this opportunity for consultancy work.

I had no idea then how God would use me in future as I was the first member of the College permanent staff establishment to study for a PhD and to complete it successfully. But use me He did. For, by then, as I have already mentioned, the College had become a School of Huddersfield Polytechnic (after its merger with the latter). Importantly, the Polytechnic was an institution which delivered degree programmes under the aegis of the Council for National Academic Awards (CNAA) but had aspirations to become independent of such academic control and to award its own degrees even at research degree level, provided it had built the necessary research capacity among its staff. So, with my PhD as a trump card, I was to play a key role in the next 18 years or so, not only in the School of Education (by promoting Educational Research) but also in the institution as a whole, through becoming the School's nominated member of the Polytechnic's Research Degrees Committee and of its Research Policy Committee at a crucial time in the process for the upgrading of the Polytechnic to a University.

Actually, almost as soon as I had succeeded in obtaining the degree of PhD, I was informed by the School/College of Education that the Equal Opportunities Commission in England (a quasi-autonomous, national government organisation which conducts formal investigations in connection with unlawful sex discrimination) was looking for a researcher to find out whether there was any discrimination against girls in getting day-release off work for part-time study. It was put to me by the School/College that I should submit a research proposal to that effect to the Commission. I had no idea of what the law said on this matter and no idea of the size of the problem in this country. Planning a Research project in these circumstances required a lot of preparation, particularly as this was a piece of policy research and was to be externally funded and monitored by officers of the Commission in their capacity as experts in the provisions of the Sex Discrimination Act 1975. But the Lord was with me for the development of the research proposal and it was accepted. The research proposal was implemented successfully. Moreover, very much beyond my expectations, two publications resulted from the project:

a)   Benett Y. and Carter D. (1981) *Sidetracked? A look at the careers advice given to Fifth-Form girls.* Equal Opportunities Commission, Manchester.

b)   Benett Y. and Carter D. (1983) *Day-release for girls.* Equal Opportunities Commission, Manchester.

The project established me as the member of the School/College staff who would take the lead in the field of Educational Research.

More research projects funded by various other agencies were to come my way. Some of the research reports were published. In particular, my work on *Professional Accountability and the maintenance of standards in vocational curricula* (Benett,1986) was a great achievement in my professional work. How did it come about? It was like this. Having read an impressive booklet in which the author developed the theme of *"Curriculum Control"* (FEU, 1981), the idea came to me to develop a research proposal about the Professional Accountability of the teaching staff in Further Education and to submit it to the Further Education Unit (Department of Education and Science). I did so and, completely unbeknown to me at the time, my proposal landed on the desk of an FEU officer who had been a former student of mine and later a colleague at the School/College of Education. The proposal was accepted and the upshot was a report which the FEU published and distributed widely within the Further Education sector. A coincidence again? I don't think so.

A further acknowledgement of the research activity that I was generating at the School/College came in an extraordinary and certainly most unexpected way, on the Friday afternoon of the 13th of July, 1984, at 5 pm. Yes, I remember the exact time and date! How can I forget: I was thinking that the next day would be my daughter's wedding and that I should be going home! However, before leaving my office I just caught sight of an air letter in the "out tray" on my desk. It was from India. I could not resist reading it there and then even at this late hour as I knew of nobody from the sub-continent who wanted to correspond with me then. The letter was about an invitation to me to present a paper at an international conference at the State University of New York in October of that year. The paper was to relate to some extent to my PhD research work. However, I did not know the person who was inviting me and wondered how she knew about my research. What I was sure of though was that, yet again, God's grace would be sufficient for me because this opportunity was unplanned. However, the invitation was not sponsored financially and I therefore had to obtain the Polytechnic's financial support for my travel expenses. Obtaining such support was not without difficulty for, seemingly, the Polytechnic authorities thought that I had wangled my way into this invitation! Yet, quite honestly, it had never even entered my head that such manoeuvring was possible in academia — how naïve I was and how I needed to learn about the ways of the world! Anyway, I did after all obtain from the Polytechnic part of the funds for my trip.

11

Into the Research fold

As indicated above, the School of Education was increasingly turning towards me for developing research proposals although I was still responsible for the running of the Diploma course. Indeed, around the mid 1980s, the message from to top (albeit, unofficially) appeared to be that the time had come for the School of Education to consider offering research degrees in Education, starting necessarily with the degree of M.Phil. The reasoning was that such a development would be particularly important for the whole Polytechnic because it was feared that it would not be sufficient for Polytechnics to wriggle themselves out of the shackles of their local Education Authorities and of the control of the CNAA, if they were to be granted university status. They (the Polytechnics) would have to meet an additional requirement which was that university status would be conditional on the Polytechnics having already been granted the power to award the research degree of MPhil and that of PhD. In the event, it took the Polytechnic of Huddersfield many years before getting to this point and I was privileged to play a part in the achievement of this goal.

How did it all happen? Well, the CNAA had been established by Royal Charter in 1964 and the purpose of this august body was the advancement of education, learning, knowledge and the arts (CNAA, 1987). The CNAA was required by its Charter to determine the conditions governing the grant of its awards whilst allowing Polytechnics and Colleges associated with it, the freedom to devise courses of a wide variety of types, having full regard to the need to maintain standards of excellence. In particular, under the terms of the Charter, the CNAA degrees were required to be comparable in standard with those of universities. Consequently, at the organisational level, the Council was empowered to approve arrangements for the registration and examination of candidates for the research degree of MPhil and for that of PhD. The Council exercised this power through its Committee for Academic Policy on the one hand, while, on the other hand, individual applications for these research degrees were considered by the Council's specialist Research Sub-Committees and their advisers. These Sub-Committees comprised College and University teachers, as well as members of research, professional and industrial organisations and, where appropriate, individual practitioners and consultants. The Council could also make arrangements for the Polytechnics' and Colleges' own Research Degrees Committees to register candidates for the Council's MPhil degree (but not yet for the PhD degree), provided that these Committees had been approved by the CNAA.

In view of the above, what I think Huddersfield Polytechnic was aiming to achieve was the establishment of its own Research Degrees Committee (under the aegis of the CNAA) in order to register MPhil candidates. But in order to obtain the Council's approval for this committee, the Polytechnic had to satisfy the Council that it had "substantial completed research", and even then, as indicated above, the Polytechnic's Research Degree Committee would have powers to register candidates for the Council's MPhil degree only (not PhD degree). However, after five years or more of a satisfactory record of exercising these powers, the Polytechnic's Research Degrees Committee could then apply to the CNAA for the delegation of further powers that would permit the registration of candidates for PhD direct and the transfer of registration from MPhil to PhD. The Polytechnic's own Research Degrees Committee would then act in all respects as an agent of the Council.

This then was the horizon for the Polytechnic's aspirations. As already mentioned, I was privileged to be the nominee of the School of Education on the Polytechnic's Research Degrees Committee, and indeed on its Research Policy Committee as well, for a number of years in the late 1980s and immediately after the Polytechnic became a University in 1992. An encouraging development within the School of Education itself was that a few other members of the staff were keen on supervising MPhil research theses and on undertaking externally-funded projects, even though my impression continued to be that Educational Research was marginalised in the School, probably because the allocation of Central Government funds for the School was for teaching on approved courses (and not for research) and for most of the staff their efforts were concentrated on delivering the Pre-Service and In-Service programmes for Initial Teacher-Training. Moreover, it was common knowledge that the amount of funding (for research activities) that the University sector received was substantially higher than the amount that the Polytechnics and Colleges sector received (DES, 1991). Nevertheless, around the late 1980s, a turn of events took place that would impact on the area of Educational Research at the Polytechnic and on my position in the School of Education. What happened was that the Rector of the Polytechnic had been appointed a member of the national Manpower Services Commission (Department of Employment). He invited a colleague and me to advise him on matters relating to Training and to Education. My task was essentially to read, highlight, comment, and advise on the issues that arose from the minutes of the meetings (of the Commission) which he received continuously. This work provided me with a great opportunity to know to some extent how the machinery of Government works in this country, and to become less intimidated by institutional, hierarchical structures! Subsequently, the Rector decided that he wanted to set up a Research Centre (within the School of Education) that would focus on researching the areas of Training and of Education, and told me that he wanted me to head that centre. This I did until I retired from full-time employment some ten years later (in 1996)

12

One more step up the career ladder

Soon after my elevation to the headship of the research centre, I was promoted to the position of Reader in the School of Education. I believe that this too was no mere coincidence. Why do I say this? Well, as I have already explained, for some years the Polytechnic had been looking ahead to getting University status and had therefore been planning for the process of taking responsibility for its own research degrees. As part of this process the Polytechnic had appointed Readers and Professors in some of its other Schools and it was now becoming necessary to create a Readership in the School of Education. But why me? What I did not know then was that (by coincidence?) one of the external advisers to the Polytechnic's Committee for the appointment of Readers and Professors had recommended my appointment as Reader, as he had been for many years the External Examiner for the Leeds University Diploma in Further Education programme which I had been directing. I can only suppose that he had seen for himself the research work which the Diploma students undertook for their dissertations and for which my team of supervisors and I were ultimately responsible. Also, by then, my experience of supervising MPhil students and that of my team had grown considerably.

My appointment as Reader boosted my confidence and it was gratifying when, soon after, a few colleagues in the School of Education came up with the proposal that the school's Research Centre should have a physical reality, in the sense of having a set of contiguous offices for the research active staff, as that arrangement would greatly facilitate day-to-day communication between us and promote dialogue. The proposal was approved by the School authorities and it was a great day when six of us moved to our adjacent rooms on the "D" floor at "Holly Bank" (short for the Holly Bank road where the School of Education was situated). With easy chairs newly upholstered and high quality, matching curtains (designed and fitted with the advice and finishing touch of our colleagues in the School's "Food and Fashion" section), and with our own logo expertly designed by our colleagues in the School's "Educational Technology" section, we were set for a fruitful future. I thank God that in the ten years or so that followed, I enjoyed enormously working at the Centre as its Head, directing many externally funded research projects and supervising a number of MPhil and PhD students. All this work contributed to the School of Education's success in the Higher Education Funding Council's Research Assessment Exercises of 1992 and 1996, respectively.

However, I still needed to learn a number of lessons! One of these was that one should not get emotionally attached to the trappings of office. I am referring to the embellishment of the Centre and of an eventful day there. I had been on an educational trip to Nigeria. I had visited various universities and seen how the infrastructure of these universities was not maintained to an appropriate standard. So, after the trip and on my way back to the Centre I stopped at the top of the stairs which led to the Centre and stood speechless in the foyer with its easy chairs, pink upholstery, greyish green window curtains and vertical blinds. I was so pleased and exhilarated and thanked God for such a congenial, well-lit, well-adorned working environment — it was such a contrast to the dark and derelict university sites that I had visited in Nigeria! However, I had to attend a meeting at the main Campus of the University some two miles away and so I made my way there. On my return, hardly an hour or so later, I again went up the stairs to the Centre and arrived at the foyer, at the top of the stairs, only to find that all the easy chairs had disappeared! I could not believe my eyes. On enquiring about what had happened I was told that the University authorities had decided that the location of the easy chairs in the foyer was in contravention of the official fire regulations. The message was clear enough. But then I wondered where the easy chairs had gone! I soon realised that my colleagues at the Centre had taken them to their own respective offices — a quick practical solution to the problem in the circumstances, I suppose! The whole event was a hard blow to my sense of self-satisfaction with my achievements so far. It was as if it was reminding me that life on this planet is ephemeral and that fundamentally these perishable, material goods do not really matter. What would last would be our research work and its impact on Education. What a lesson!/

Another lesson which I drew from my line of business was the wide range of prevailing perspectives on Education within the Polytechnic, particularly colleagues' perspectives on students' learning during their placements for work experience in industry and commerce. I became aware of these different perspectives during my meetings with colleagues from the other Schools of the Polytechnic, in my capacity as a member of the research team for two CNAA funded Research and Development projects. The projects were respectively about the assessment and self-assessment of undergraduate Polytechnic students at the workplace. I gained the impression that occasionally the projects engendered some tension between myself (as one inclined to think in terms of Educational principles that underpin learning) and those team members whose interest was in the practical aspects of work-based learning. The upshot of this tension was that I was asked by the team to explain my theoretical position in a paper. I agreed to do so and this compelled me to think deeply on the whole issue of work-based learning. The outcome was beyond all expectations: not only was my paper published in a national, refereed, academic journal but it also won a place as a chapter in an Open University's "reader" for its *MA Course in Education* programme (see Murphy, 1999).

Yet another lesson which I had to learn, during this period of heightened activity in my professional life, was that it was not enough to have novel ideas and to take the initiative in implementing them without the continual personal commitment of time and energy to see them through to the end. For example, I had the idea of experimenting with the concept of **Mentoring** for young adults, with the School of Education Pre-Service student teachers as Mentors. I thought that the School was well placed to provide such Mentors to a group of some ten ethnic minority, unemployed, youngsters who were on a vocational training course that was funded by the Manpower Services Commission. The Mentors would thus be mature students with considerable practical experience of working in industry, commerce and administration. They would benefit from the process through helping the youngsters, on a one-to-one basis, with their (the youngsters') studies, and gaining a deeper understanding of teaching and learning, and of Guidance and Counselling for the young. The idea was formally accepted by the School and a programme based on this idea and funded by the local Training and Enterprise Council (TEC) was mounted. However, the programme soon had to be discontinued for a number of reasons. Among these was the impossibility of finding a sufficient number of work placements locally for the youngsters. Another reason was my inability to cope with putting in place this innovative training system whilst, at the same time, launching in this country (at the behest of the School) an innovative MEd programme specifically tailored to the needs of educationists from developing countries.

13

Outward bound

After such a wounding experience was it really possible for me to continue to believe with St. Paul "that in all things God works with those... whom He has called according to His purpose" (Romans 8: 28)? Yes, it was. The reason is that the development of an MEd programme of study which targeted the Third World countries would provide a new direction to my course of action in the years that followed and enable me to see God's blessing in my professional life in new, unbelievable, ways. The crux of the matter was that the CNAA's (1987) regulations had imposed certain stringent conditions on providing a taught course at Master's degree level. One of these regulations was that any proposal for a course at that level had to be based upon a team of staff who had not only themselves engaged in advanced studies or in research (in the field of study for the proposal) but who continued to be actively involved in research, development and/or other relevant activities. In view of this, the problem that I faced was that as leader of the team for the proposed MEd course, I had not undertaken any research activities in developing countries since I went to India some 15 years earlier and, as far as I knew, my colleagues in the team had not either, although some had been running short, taught courses, in developing countries. The difficulty was that such educational research in developing countries, particularly fieldwork (as this would help to back up our MEd proposal with concrete educational data), would be a costly affair and was not, I guess, a priority in the financial plan for the allocation of resources within the School of Education.

However, as often in the past, help was at hand for I was soon commissioned by the British Government's Overseas Development Administration (ODA) to evaluate the implementation of the World Bank/ODA funded *Industrial Schools Project* in Turkey in 1990. This sponsored piece of evaluation research was just the impetus needed at the time to position my career in an outward bound direction for the rest of my working life. Indeed, other externally funded projects were to follow. For example, I recall one afternoon, in 1994, arriving back at the School campus, after having visited another institution with a colleague, and just as we got out of the car, the Head of the School's International Office rushed towards us. He said that he had received a telephone call from the International Labour Office (ILO), in Turin, about the recruitment of Education consultants for a short-term consultancy in Ghana, where the University of Cape Coast was launching an ILO/UNDP funded programme for the research degree of MPhil in the area of *Vocational Training for Entrepreneurship*. My colleagues and I were presented with such an opportunity that we simply had to accept the invitation to apply for the consultancy. Thus it was that three of us from the School went to lecture for a few weeks on the taught part of the MPhil programme, and it fell on me, subsequently, to supervise the students' MPhil dissertations and to advise the Head of the Vocational Training Department at the University of Cape Coast about a Tracer Study of its graduates. Actually, the Technical and Vocational Education and Training system in Ghana was not unknown to me because previously, I had gone to Ghana to advise on the Upgrading of its Polytechnics, on the invitation of a former Diploma student who had been elevated to the position of Director of Technical Education in the country.

As far as possible and even after my retirement I have tried to maintain my professional contacts with educationists in other developing countries too, and surprises such as the following were welcomed. The surprise came from a former South African MEd student. He invited me to attend the conference of the International Association of Community and Further Education Colleges on *International Collaboration in Community and Further Education and Training ___ a strategy for the new millennium,* at Cape Town, in the year 2000, and to chair the sessions on the Opening Day. Gratifying too was that I was presented, at an after dinner ceremony, with the "Award of Excellence" for my "Contribution to Education and Training".

Projects in developing countries such as those above, though important, came my way only intermittently. However, in parallel with them, a relationship with one particular Third World country had begun to develop which would be effective in providing more opportunities for educational research. To give a brief account of what happened, around the late 1980s, I kept receiving telephone calls from one of my former students. He was from The Gambia. He had attended our Advanced Diploma in Further Education course some ten years before and whilst back home had kept in touch with me. He was now a high-ranking officer in the Ministry of Education of his country and would constantly ask me to visit his country. He would reassure me that his country was developing fast, mentioning specially the new telecommunications system recently installed and the expansion of tourism. Thus it was that Evelyn and I went on holiday to The Gambia for the first time in 1988, instead of going to the traditional holiday resorts in Europe as in the previous years. And what a welcome we had! To see my former student together with another former student standing on the tarmac where the aircraft had landed, dressed in their typically large African robes and waiting to greet us at the foot of the steps was truly wonderful; and it was also pleasing to be invited to a dinner party with them and with the British Education consultants who were at the time reviewing the country's policy for Education.

This first visit marked the beginning of an on-going professional relationship with my former Gambian students and subsequently with educational institutions in the country. I was confident that The Lord was continuing to bless me in wonderful ways as this window of opportunities opened for me; and I started to feel even more outward bound for the Third World when, one Sunday afternoon (a year or two later), the telephone rang at about 1pm (the very time when Evelyn and I were, as usual, having a short nap at home after the Sunday lunch). It was the same former Gambian student and friend on the line. He told me that the Vice-President of The Gambia (who was also the Minister of Education at the time) wanted to talk to me there and then on the phone. I had met the latter briefly when I had paid a courtesy visit to the Ministry of Education during my first trip to The Gambia. The Vice-President now wondered if we could host his twin teenage daughters for two years, as they progressed in their Sixth Form studies in this country. In the event, Evelyn and I welcomed the two girls in our home. This initial relationship with the Gambians was to give me some valuable insights into the socio-economic and educational needs of the Less Developed Countries (LDCs).

A further reinforcement of my feeling that my educational activities were now bound up with the development of education in Third World countries was to follow when some years later, in 1994, quite "out of the blue", I got a letter inviting me to give the keynote address at the International Conference of ERNWACA (Educational Research Network for West And Central Africa) on the *"Harmonisation of Transnational Research Projects"*. The letter was from the ERNWACA National Co-ordinator for The Gambia, as that country was hosting the conference that year. The significance of this invitation (in terms of my professional work) was that it brought me straightaway into contact with researchers in Education from 12 countries (mostly, francophone) in West Africa, and with Education Consultants from two key donor countries for that region, namely, the USA and Canada. Indeed, later on, I was given the key role of touring five of these countries to monitor and evaluate the progress which they were making with the research projects that these international donors were funding. The outcome of this demanding activity was a substantial contribution to the production of the ERNWACA (2002) report entitled *Transnational view of Basic Education: issues of Access, Quality, and Community Participation in West and Central Africa,* and published by USAID/SARA. Moreover, a few years later (in the year 2000), and again "out of the blue", I received a telephone call from one of the Education Consultants for ERNWACA. He invited me to review the intervention of the USA-based *CARE International* (a Non-Governmental Organisation) in Education, in the francophone country of Mali. This I did and enjoyed thoroughly my meetings with the officials of the local schools and with those of the Parent-Teacher Associations, particularly at Macina (in the region of Ségou), and at Timbuktu.

My association with ERNWACA soon earned me the position of "Scientific Adviser" to the network's Gambia Chapter. As such, and with Evelyn's help (in Statistics and Computing), I have been able to date to bring my research experience to bear on a number of projects in The Gambia, such as, the evaluation of the Government's *Scholarship Trust Fund for Secondary School girls in rural areas*, the *Gambia College Institutional Review, the study of Parent-Teacher Associations at Lower Basic/Primary schools* and the *Measurement of change in mature students' knowledge of the Built Environment.* Indeed, my consultancy work in The Gambia has extended beyond research sponsored by the Government of The Gambia and has included research projects (in Education) funded by *UNICEF*, by *UNESCO* and by *ACTION AID* (Gambia), respectively.

14

Conclusion

It seems necessary in concluding this short autobiography to reiterate that it does not claim to be a piece of academic writing and/or to be of philosophical or theological or scientific interest. As I have explained in Section 1, what I have tried to do is to provide a brief narrative of my life that, I hope, brings glory to our Father God and lends some plausibility to the proposition that He does intervene in the affairs of men. My approach has been to tackle this theme head on by concentrating on just a few events, often initiated by unexpected phone calls, but there have been many other events which, like these, defeat any rational explanation and yet have not been included. Indeed, the sampled events represent only a small fraction of the totality of events throughout my adult life that could, arguably, be construed as supporting the proposition. This is not surprising given that my professional experience has been wide-ranging. In point of fact, I have not referred to my experiences as, Editor of the British Journal entitled *The Vocational Aspect of Education,* and as Visiting Professor of Education at the Bolton Institute.

It also seems necessary to reiterate what I have said in my introductory section about my awareness of God's continuous presence in my life, even when I have drifted away from Him. It has been very much like what the psalmist says, that is, "I am always aware of the Lord's presence; He is near, and nothing can shake me" (Ps16:8). But whilst David could only suppose that if he "flew away beyond the east or lived in the farthest place in the west", God would be there to lead him and to help him, I can affirm that in all my travels across the continents, I have always felt secure in the knowledge that God was everywhere with me, in the sense that the Holy Spirit who indwells me, relates me to Him, and turns my groans into prayer (Romans 8:26-27). What I mean is that, in Billy Graham's (1978) words, the Holy Spirit has been "in fellowship" with me. He has "entered my life". It is a mystery: and this mystery is well expressed in S⁺ Paul's stupendous declaration that God gives life to our mortal bodies by the presence of His Spirit in us (Romans 8:11). I expect this staggering concept of God's "personal disclosure of Himself to humankind" (Green, 2002), abiding in us by the Spirit which He has given us (1John 3:24), will be denigrated as foolish by those who put their faith only in analytical reasoning and/or in empirical evidence to get to the truth about everything. Quite clearly too, this profound mystery subverts the ways in which some people hope of "experiencing the Divine within" (Lucas, 1996) by, for example, taking mind-changing drugs and/or practising transcendental meditation (perhaps as a consequence of disillusion with the hollow philosophies of the secular world). For my part, I rest my case on the reassuring words of Scripture that the Holy Spirit's "presence" is shown in some way in each person for the good of all" (1Cor. 12:7). I acknowledge that the tantalising question for me has been: how do I find out about that way? The reply that springs to mind is that God's promise is expressed in no uncertain words thus:

"I will teach you the way you should go
I will instruct you and advise you" (Ps 32:8)

Far from me even to attempt to unravel the complexities of the ways by which God's will for His world and for each person is being played out. But complex they are, if one is to accept the proposition of "process theology" that "God both influences and is influenced by the world" and that "God is always offering to each occasion an ideal possibility for the future" which is derived from "the divine vision of possibilities" (Clements-Jewery, 2005). On the other hand, there is the relatively simple distinction which Stott (1992) makes, between God's "general" will (for all Christians, in all places, at all times), and His "particular" will (for particular people, at particular places, at particular times). The former is revealed in the Bible and is that, as Christians, we "should be conformed to the likeness of His Son" (Romans 8:29). The latter is not revealed as such in the Bible, as His will is different for each person, both in matters spiritual and in matters secular (such as in the choice of a career or of a life partner). However, there are guidelines in the "good book" that point to how we are meant to discover God's "particular" will for each of us. For example, one guideline is that the Christian must be willing to give in to God's purpose and to pray expectantly, for it is through his/her communion with God that God's will is revealed (Romans 12:2). Another guideline is that he/she should seek advice (from wise people, including his/her parents), weigh up the pros and cons, and wait before making any decision.

My trilogy of faith

As for me, I can testify to the absolutely wonderful peace that comes with knowing that one is doing God's will. In spite of the ferocity of the devil's attack on my spirit (even during morning prayers when sometimes memories come flooding back and/or my mind starts wandering over my plans for the day), I have experienced the peace that Jesus promised (John14:27), by putting my trust in Him. I have never lost the sense of wonder at His "amazing grace" for such an undeserving one as me, and I have been sustained spiritually by what I might call my trilogy of faith, that is, three themes from the New Testament, each represented by key verses as follows:

Theme	Key verses
God is Spirit:	*"God is a Spirit, and they that worship Him must worship Him in spirit and in truth." (John 4:24; 1 Timothy 6:16).*
God loves us:	*"For God so loved the world, that He gave His only begotten Son" (John3:16; Romans 8:39).*
God knows our needs:	*"Your Father already knows what you need before you ask Him" (Matthew 6:8;32).*

Like Horsfall (2006), I have concluded that once I had taken God at His word, I was no longer "straining to earn His favour". Instead, I could "lean on Him" at all times, "bask in His acceptance", "delight in His forgiveness" and "rest in His unchanging love". This is not to say that I am not aware of some inescapable questions about, for example, the history of Christendom, the existence and nature of God and of evil, and the origin of life on earth, let alone the origin of the universe! As a matter of fact, I am impressed by the splendid successes of the physical sciences; and I find the analytic method of reasoning (with its reduction of complex problems to their constituent parts) to be very much to my liking. Also, I agree that "it is for us, as Christians, to perceive the hand of God at work in the sciences" and "to be learning truth from every genuine science" (Ramsay, 1977). However, I am inclined to the view that religious truth is not amenable to scientific analysis because religion is not an objectively rational undertaking independent of personal faith. As a man of faith, what I can say, in ending, is that although "I cannot tell why He, whom angels worship, should set his love upon the sons of men" (Fullerton, 1857-1932) and that I do not know why God's "wondrous grace" has been made known to me (Whittle, 1840-1901), nevertheless, "I know whom I have believed" (2 Timothy 1:12) for He has intervened in my life and all the time I have been learning to live with mystery and vicissitudes but also with "amazing grace".

References

Anderson N (1984) *Christianity and World Religions – the challenge of pluralism.* Inter-Varsity Press. Leicester. England.

Barclay W (1977) *In the hands of God.* Collins. Fount Paperbacks. Glasgow.

Benett Y (1966) *Curriculum and syllabuses in the primary schools of Mauritius.* MA thesis. University of London.

Bryman A (1988) *Quantity and Quality in Social Research.* Routledge, London.

Buber M (1947) *Between man and man.* Kegan Paul. London.

Clements-Jewery P (2005) *Intercessory Prayer.* Ashgate, Aldershot, England.

Coulson C (1966) *Science and Christian belief.* Collins Fontana books. London.

Curtis S (1965) *Introduction to the Philosophy of Education.* University Tutorial Press Ltd, Foxton, England.

Department of Education and Science (1991) *Higher Education – A new Framework.* HMSO. London.

Fielding N and Fielding J (1986) *Linking Data.* Qualitative Research Methods Series. SAGE publications, London.

Further Education Unit (1981) *Curriculum Control.* Department of Education and Science. London.

Gadamer H-G (1976) *Philosophical Hermeneutics.* University of California Press. Los Angeles. USA.

Gulhati R (1990) *The making of economic policy in Africa.* Economic Development Institute of the World Bank. Washington DC.

Habermas J (1988) *On the logic of the Social Sciences.* Polity Press. Cambridge. UK.

Hawkins P (1988) A Phenomenological Psychodrama Workshop. In Reason P.(Ed) *Human Inquiry in Action.* SAGE publications, London.

Heiler F (1958) *Prayer. History and Psychology.* Galaxy Book. Oxford University Press.

Hicks P (1998) *Evangelicals and Truth.* Apollos. Leicester, England.

Hicks P (2000) *What could I say?* Inter-Varsity Press, Leicester, England.

Horsfall T (2006) Love's resting place. In *New Daylight, 15th February, 2006.* Bible Reading Fellowship. Oxford

Husserl E (1970) *Logical Investigations.* University Printing House. Cambridge. England.

Inhelder B and Piaget J (1958) *The growth of logical thinking.* Routledge and Kegan Paul. London.

Kirk J, and Miller M, (1986) *Reliability and Validity in Qualitative Research..* SAGE publications, London.

Lennon D (2003) Beauty in weakness In *Encounter with God, 25th September, 2003.* Scripture Union. Milton Keynes. UK.

Lenoir P and Brunel H (1974) *Mauritius: Isle de France en mer indienne.* Translation by Henri Brunel. Editions Isle de France, Port-Louis, Mauritius.

Lucas E (1996) *Science and the New Age challenge.* APOLLOS. Leicester.

Lyotard J-F (1999) *The Postmodern Condition: a report on knowledge.* Manchester University Press.

Merriam S (1988) *Case Study Research in Education.* Jossey-Bass. San Francisco. USA.

Morris B (1959) Sigmund Freud In Judges A *The function of teaching.* Faber and Faber. London.

Moustakas C (1994) *Phenomenological Research Methods.* SAGE publications, London.

Murphy P (Ed) (1999) *Learners, Learning and Assessment.* SAGE Publications. London.

Piaget J (1950) *The psychology of intelligence.* Routledge and Kegan Paul. London.

Pollard D (1998) *Why do they do that?* Lion Publishing plc. Oxford, England.

Popkewitz T (1984) *Paradigm and Ideology in Educational Research.* The Falmer Press. London.

Popper K (1972) *The Logic of Scientific Discovery.* Hutchinson. London.

Ramsay M (1977) The Spirit and the Gospel of St John In Ramsay M and Suenens L J. *Come Holy Spirit.* Darton, Longman and Todd. London.

Reid A (1961) *Ways of Knowledge and Experience.* George Allen and Unwin, London.

Sapsford R and Jupp V (1996) *Data Collection and Analysis.* SAGE publications. London.

Schultz A (1971) *The problem of social reality.* Collected Papers I. Martinus Nijhoff. The Hague.

Smith P (2000) Philosophy of Science and its relevance for the Social Sciences In Burton D. (Ed) *Research Training for Social Scientists.* SAGE Publications. London.

Stevenson N (2000) Questions of Hermeneutics: Beyond Empiricism and Post-modernism In Burton D. (Ed) *Research Training for Social Scientists.* SAGE publications, London.

Stott J (1992) *The Contemporary Christian.* Inter-Varsity Press, Leicester, England.

Strauss R (1993) *Mauritius, Réunion and Seychelles.* Lonely Planet Publications. London.

Usher R, Bryant I and Johnston R (1997) *Adult Education and the Post-modern Challenge.* Routledge, London.

Wright C (1974) *Mauritius.* Davis and Charles (Holdings) Limited. Newton Abbot. Devon. England.

ISBN 1425116841